Naval Warfare Today and Tomorrow

ENDPAPER

As dawn breaks over the South Atlantic on 20 April 1982, Royal Marines line up for a weapons check on board HMS *Hermes*, flagship of the British Falkland Islands Task Force. Tightly packed Sea Harriers and Sea King helicopters are in the background. The picture gives some idea of an aircraft carrier's multi-purpose capability even though *Hermes* herself had only a limited capability in the aircraft operating role. (Press Association)

Naval Warfare Today and Tomorrow

HUBERT MOINEVILLE

translation and picture captions by
Commander P. R. Compton-Hall

Basil Blackwell

First published in French as *La guerre navale*

This edition first published 1983
Basil Blackwell Publisher Limited
108 Cowley Road, Oxford OX4 1JF, England

British Library Cataloguing in Publication Data

Moineville, Hubert
Naval warfare today and tomorrow.
1. Sea power—Europe 2. Europe—Military policy
I. Title II. Compton-Hall, Richard
III. La guerre navale. *English*
359'.03'094 VA450

ISBN 0-631-13253-8
ISBN 0-631-13291-0 Pbk

Typesetting by Pioneer, East Sussex
Printed in Great Britain by Billing and Sons, Worcester

CONTENTS

	Author's note	vii
	Introduction	1
Part I	The Possibilities of Naval Confrontation Today	5
1	War and humanity	7
2	The role of a naval arm	13
3	The place of naval operations today	17
Part II	The General Characteristics and Context of Naval Operations	29
4	General characteristics of operations	31
5	Naval warfare and nuclear weapons	37
6	Territories, commercial assets at sea and naval warfare	46
Part III	Development of the Forces and Naval Strategy	49
7	Development of the participants in naval warfare	51
8	The consequences for naval strategy	76
	Appendix to part III	86
Part IV	Some Thoughts on the Conduct of Naval Action	89
9	Choices to be made in advance	91
10	Basic options at the start of operations	103
11	Problems of naval operations	110
	Conclusion	128
	Postscript: The Falklands War	131

PLATE SECTION

Between pp. 88 and 89;
captions by Commander P. R. Compton-Hall.

AUTHOR'S NOTE

The opinions expressed in this book reflect my personal view of specific questions concerning naval strategy, and I am solely responsible for these opinions. However, I have received much advice and assistance in formulating them. Those who have generously helped me in this way will, no doubt, recognize their contribution and I should like them to accept my deepest gratitude.

INTRODUCTION

The sea, as much as the land, is a place where man seeks to prove his strength. While from the earliest times the sea has been used for fishing and for transport, it has always been a field of battle too.

The tools used for fighting at sea gradually evolved into warships. After centuries of maritime history these ships have become diversified and complex systems representing most of today's technological capabilities. In order to be militarily effective, they are provided with a whole range of aircraft, methods of detection ranging from ocean-bed sensors to orbiting satellites, the means of processing and transmitting data at high speed and, of course, all the logistic support necessary for employing them as military instruments at sea. For convenience, I will refer to all these things together simply as the naval arm. (Similarly, actions will be termed 'naval' whether they take place on, under or above the surface and whether or not the combatants are all ships.)

The component parts of a naval system are so numerous and so costly that no nation can possess them in their entirety. Each country seeks to discern its defence requirements and provide itself with a navy which is capable of fulfilling these within its limitations. As a result, the navies of the world are surprisingly varied, as much in their composition as in the characteristics of their individual components. The rapidity of evolution that characterizes modern technology continually adds to the complexity and diversification of weapon systems, propulsion, design and construction. In the 35 years since the last great naval war, the hardware has made spectacular progress:

revolutionary innovations such as nuclear propulsion and the military use of space have made their appearance. Other advances of no less importance are confidently predicted that would have been unimaginable a few years ago.

In view of these dramatic changes, it is hard to imagine what a major confrontation at sea would now be like. Is such a confrontation even conceivable? It might seem not, for a balance has apparently been reached between the major powers. It is based on the threat of strategic nuclear weapons which deter military action by one power against another. And it happens that the powers with such weapons are also those that possess major fleets which could by themselves fight a large-scale war at sea.

However, the theory of deterrence, which brings about something of a military stalemate wherever it applies, is accompanied elsewhere by a proliferation of force involving countries disputing their own rights or those of the great powers; and those countries even invite the great powers to assist when it is believed that they can do so without risk of escalation. Force has so far been used in this way at just about every level and scale of violence except nuclear war; and that includes naval participation.

The range of conceivable naval confrontations has thus been greatly extended with respect to the political-strategic situations from which confrontations can arise, to their level of violence and to the systems employed. The whole business is so complicated and the conceivable situations so varied that we should like to throw some light on the subject in order to see more clearly how and where naval confrontations might take place today and in the future. That is the purpose of this book.

A study of the problem must be objective if it is to have any value. The arguments that follow are therefore general and are not related to any particular players in the continuing world-wide naval game. In particular, it must be stressed that they have no special bearing on plans for the French navy which the author has served. Furthermore, the conclusions offer no single ready-made solution directly applicable to any specific problem. However, they aim to establish facts and to offer ideas and arguments that may help to clarify specific situations. Some of these arguments may be original; but the main endeavour has been to collect, relate and discuss widely expressed ideas. Although the facts are, strictly, relevant to 1980, they have a considerable bearing on the future and will, I hope, to some extent illuminate the road ahead.

At the outset, it is worth asking a practical question: where, today, could a naval war occur while a balance of strategic nuclear power exists? The answer is sought in the first part of this book, which consists of a theoretical survey, taking as its starting point the origins of conflicts and looking not only at actual warfare but, as far as possible, at the entire gamut of conceivable naval confrontations. The second part examines more fully and concretely everything that is the essence of a naval operation: the general characteristics conferred by its environment; the conceptual context conferred by nuclear weapons whose role goes beyond that of a simple weapons system; and the physical context of naval operations, comprising territories and commercial assets at sea. In the third part the actors themselves are studied as they appear on the maritime stage, in order to see how their evolution during the past 35 years has changed the whole character of naval confrontations and will, perhaps, change it even more in the future. The final part seeks to draw some conclusions about the actual conduct of naval operations.

Part I

The Possibilities of Naval Confrontation Today

In view of the changes that have taken place during the past 35 years, and in particular the concept of strategic deterrence, what are the possibilities of a confrontation at sea today? It is impossible to answer this question without first considering the place of naval operations in warfare generally. To start with, it might be useful to look at the principal characteristics of war itself so that these can be used as instruments for further analysis.

1

WAR AND HUMANITY

Warfare persists throughout the world. What is its place in the life of mankind? What, in fact, is war? Why is the human race perpetually at war with itself? Most great philosophies have tried to resolve this paradox. Their answers have been varied and contradict each other on many issues, but on one thing they appear to agree: the causes of war are deep-rooted in the very nature of mankind. This suggests that war is an ingrained characteristic of humanity, and that it will never be eradicated by law, convention or government, nor by a careful balance of power among nations. Although the era of the nuclear deterrent has kept the great powers at bay and appears to ensure that there will never be another global confrontation, the evidence of the world around us gives few grounds for hoping that war will be wholly eliminated.

What does war comprise? The subject has become so complex that it might be helpful to consider first, on a deliberately schematic basis, what its basic ingredients are. For a start, it can be said that war consists of an *organized group* using *violence* to achieve an *objective*. Violence is the most obvious characteristic, although it admits of several levels and may be potential rather than actual. An organized group may be as small in scale as a group of pirates or a political organization indulging in terrorism at sea. For simplicity, however, the term is taken here to mean a nation centred on a government, although other circumstances can certainly be envisaged. (Certain types of action, such as terrorism at sea and piracy, are therefore not treated here.)

An objective is a rather more complicated notion. It would normally be, or at least appear to be, rational in so far as it is based on expectations of gaining something despite the risks implicit in warfare; and it assumes that success in achieving that end will be more likely through war than by other methods. Objectives may also be, or appear to be, irrational. People may go to war in order to satisfy an impulse that evades all attempts at rational evaluation and for which we must perhaps seek an explanation in the congenital characteristics of mankind. Nevertheless, even a war engendered by irrational expectations may, if it involves national organizations, assume in practice an aspect very similar to that of a rational war. This book will be confined mainly to 'rational' warfare. At the same time it should be remembered that there are always some irrational factors in war and that warfare is an activity in which there will inevitably be a degree of uncertainty.

If we turn now to the practice of war, we see that wars are declared and become organized in order to achieve aims that define an objective. These aims may well be no more than apparent and secondary in relation to more deep-rooted causes, but they are nevertheless seen as the logical base for all the talk and all the action that war engenders. We need therefore to look at them with some care. The reasons and justifications for going to war fill volumes of historical writing. I do not propose to list them, but in order to examine the possibilities of naval confrontation I think it useful to establish the three separate headings under which the aims of war can invariably be classified: predacity; the pursuit of power; and concern for security.

Predacity, or expansion, whether acknowledged as an aim or not, may relate to an isolated resource or to the acquisition of a whole territory in so far as this can be the provider of several resources, including space. (For a long time, incidentally, one of the major objects of expansion derived from the collection, shipment and marketing of human slaves, and one would like to be able to say that this kind of expansion has disappeared.)

The pursuit of power can take many forms. It can be the wholly explicit ambition of annexing another country. It can also consist, rather less obviously, of setting up a government that is ostensibly national but over which strict control may be exercised. It may proceed, too, through a wide variety of dealings and pressures designed to ensure that control is achieved.

Concern for security may again be either genuine or simply a screen for something else. It can be manifested in a broad range of actions — assuming a strategic position, for instance, or inhibiting the development of a competing nation's power by destroying one of its resources or by the pre-emptive destruction of part of its military forces.

The methods and procedures a warring nation adopts to achieve the objectives put forward by its government may assume widely different forms. But in the end all these serve only to herald, to prepare or to undertake actions that consist basically of destroying or at least neutralizing the enemy and, if possible, capturing people, assets or military forces. It is the ability to destroy, neutralize or capture that is the ultimate criterion of effectiveness for any method of waging war: this point will recur many times in what is to follow.

In general it can be said that effectiveness depends on the degree of violence, or of potential violence, displayed — a concept that has become all the more forceful with the appearance of nuclear weapons which so prodigiously enlarge the scale of our destructive capabilities. There are many different levels of violence, and we may conveniently think of them as steps on a ladder. For example, two steps traditionally considered to be at opposite ends of the ladder are the firing of the first shot and the use of a nuclear weapon.

Using these few basic principles we can draw up a very simplified table of confrontations. Warlike confrontations can be classified by their *intensity* and by their *duration*. These two factors — associated with the objectives, the means available and the levels of violence which have just been examined — serve as keys for establishing a summary classification.

The bottom rung of the intensity ladder is peace. In fact, in the state of the world today, and in that unprotected space that is the sea, peace does not really exist. The word is used, mainly as a linguistic convenience, to describe the permanent state of tension in which we live; while this does not yet amount to a confrontation, the notion of confrontation already governs much of our behaviour. However, in order to be quite clear about the bottom rung of the intensity ladder, it is fair to say it begins with a state of tension which is low at first and then becomes more and more serious until crisis level is reached. At that stage it is a question of bloodless confrontation or one in which the use of force is at least strictly limited. The existence of the nuclear deterrent is highly significant in certain kinds of confrontation, but crises can also arise without any nuclear implications. They involve actions that are as widespread and complex as many wartime operations. A period of crisis is also characterized by intense political arguments. Crisis can, by itself, lead to the achievement of an objective, but it can also result in war.

War is manifested at first in its limited form. Limited war is a conflict that is directed at only some of the aims that have been suggested. It allows the use of certain methods to be withheld and it is bound by a degree of rationality.[1] Above limited war and at the top of the intensity ladder comes total war. This is an all-out war with multiple objectives in which every means available is employed. Its intention is completely to destroy the opposition as a nation organized according to a certain pattern. Today, it is hardly conceivable that a nuclear nation would engage in total war without the extensive use of nuclear weapons, since it is unlikely that, given such an objective and possessing such weapons, it would deny itself their use; and the declared military doctrines of certain great powers confirm this. By reason of its own excesses, such an enterprise could not be regarded as entirely rational; none the less its spectre permanently hovers over East—West relations.

The second key to a classification of confrontations is duration. It is, of course, self-evident that a war may be long or short; but the expressions 'a long war' and 'a short war' are not precisely defined. Most people would think a war was long if it lasted several years, and short if it was over in a few days, but there is a hazy area between the two. In practice, the idea of a short (non-nuclear) war is generally associated with the availability of only small quantities of armaments or of military

[1] The Anglo-Argentinian conflict of 1982 in the Falkland Islands illustrated perfectly this kind of naval warfare. There will frequently be references which are relevant to it in this book. The postscript offers a number of observations about the Falklands conflict along the lines of thought developed in the text.

personnel. But that is only a very rough approximation. Total nuclear war is also associated in most minds with a short war, on the grounds that the destruction following a nuclear exchange would be such that the conflict would extinguish itself like a fire that burns itself out. However, this assumption might be thought over-hasty. In the first place a nuclear exchange could be preceded by operations of varying degrees of intensity over an indeterminate period; secondly, it is possible for a nuclear exchange to be interrupted — along the lines foreseen by the American flexible response or by a final warning of an independent deterrent like the French *force-de-frappe*, for example. Finally, there are, after all, techniques for continuing war in a nuclear environment which could certainly be improved still further.

However that may be, one should not forget that everybody at the beginning of the last two world wars reckoned that the war could only be short. But both lasted a long time because it was found that, by digging in instead of standing up and fighting in the open along traditional lines, armies could hold out against machine guns; tanks and aeroplanes could be countered by anti-tank and anti-aircraft weapons; and government could survive under the bombs.

For want of anything better we are left with the rather trite but none the less valid thought that both long and short wars are equally conceivable and that, in particular, classification by duration is not identical with classification by intensity.

Summarizing these reflections on the part played by war in human life, we can state that they lead to the following conclusions:

1 The phenomenon of war arises from causes so deep-rooted that one cannot hope to eradicate it permanently by deterrence, despite its present effectiveness.
2 War consists of an organized group using force (a government, so far as this discussion is concerned) with a view to achieving an objective which amounts to predacity, the assumption of power or concern for security.
3 In practice, war proceeds by destroying, neutralizing or capturing people, assets or military forces, in each case using the appropriate level of violence.

The foregoing points permit warlike confrontations to be classed (1) by degrees of intensity — that is to say, by a state of tension, by a crisis preceding war itself, then by limited war and finally by total war; and (2) by duration — for a long war or a short war — which does not necessarily coincide with the degree of intensity. Such are the schematics of war in general which will help to illuminate the following considerations about naval warfare specifically.

2

THE ROLE OF A NAVAL ARM

Within the general phenomenon of war the proper role of a naval arm must now be determined, before we go on to examine the possibilities of a confrontation at sea.

The naval component has a special place in the armed services because, after all, since man is not aquatic, the life and heart of a nation are on land. The naval forces are thus less universally, less intimately involved with normal human activity than are land forces: it is clear, for example, that their ability to effect capture is severely limited. An examination of the naval role involves looking first at what can give the sea a share in war operations that belong essentially to the land; then isolating what constitutes the proper sphere of naval action; and finally identifying exactly what are the stakes in a battle at sea.

In the case of naval operations in support of land warfare, the final outcome will be determined by the effectiveness of troops fighting on shore. They can be assisted by sea in various ways:

1 The transporting of troops from one land mass to another. This greatly extends an army's ability to manoeuvre and makes sea transport an important and even decisive element in strategic planning.
2 The disembarkation of a landing force from troop transports. Today this operation requires specialized methods of landing either by water or by air.
3 Fire support for troops ashore. This can be given directly by ships' gunnery or indirectly by aircraft carried on board. Fire support from seaward is particularly valuable for a landing

operation when all the land-support weapons are not yet established on site, or for backing up a distant operation for which land-based aircraft cannot be provided in sufficient quantity.

4 Especially for distant operations, the sea is often the only means of ensuring heavy logistic support for troops ashore.

It should be noted that battles between forces may be necessary to ensure freedom of action for the power that wishes to mount an amphibious operation. This will be discussed later with regard to the concept of 'control of the sea'.

The other possibility for a naval arm is what could be called purely naval action. This may be an action joined by one naval element against another seagoing element, whether military or not, or an autonomous action undertaken by a naval element against the land — that is, independently of shore support for the army — and consequently using fire power. It is a combination of purely naval actions that brings about a truly naval war. In particular this includes attacking and defending merchant ships whose importance to the world can only grow, as will be seen later.

Control of the sea will also be included under the heading of purely naval action. A simple definition is impractical because it concerns a fluctuating state of affairs whose parameters can vary enormously. Control of the sea is a kind of substitute for the advantages on land of possessing a territory: one is on home ground there; one is kept informed; one's own laws are applied; it gives one maximum freedom of action; and it can provide the best possible facilities if the use of force becomes necessary. At sea there is no question of going so far, for a multiplicity of reasons which will be stressed when we come to examine more closely the forms that naval operations can take. One can nevertheless achieve, at least temporarily and in a specific area, the freedom of action which is the aim of control of the sea. The requirements are to have sufficient information about what is happening within the given area, where there is neither a civil population nor a police force to co-operate, and to be able to intervene in the area with a force which is sufficiently effective to hunt down, quickly, any possible opponents. At this stage control of the sea therefore implies defensive action. In other respects being the first 'at home' in the area confers considerable tactical advantages – hence the advantage of maintaining a presence, or even an ostensible presence, not only in war but at all times.

In order to clarify the complex range of actions whose theatre may be the sea, some common denominators must be found. These might be called 'the naval warfare stakes'; and they will serve as a guide throughout our subsequent analysis.

It goes without saying that the different types of naval action (which will be listed briefly) have seen throughout history, because of the development of new techniques and the diversity of circumstances, enormous variations in their forms, their power, their geographical span and, in short, their capacity for influencing the outcome of a war. The diversity of these naval actions is too great for them to constitute criteria for an easy evaluation of naval forces' capacities in the confrontations conceivable today. But it seems that the stakes involved in naval actions could conveniently be put into three categories which appear to be sufficiently fundamental for there always to be at least one of them that applies, and for the three to cover among them every case.

The first possible stake is territory. If naval action wins this stake through the intermediary of landing troops, it indirectly uses all the procedures of war: destruction, neutralization and capture. If a purely naval action is involved, it is largely limited to surface weapons and therefore to the capacity to destroy. But more significantly it could today, with ship-borne aircraft and, above all, missiles, *destroy* the very heart of continents – on the condition, of course, that the necessary weapons are in play.

The second permanent stake consists of mankind's assets at sea. The first and oldest is the merchant vessel. It has been, since the dawn of civilization, an essential agent of commerce, barter and consequently of development; and its role continues to grow alongside that of the aeroplane. For example, from 1964 to 1979 the tonnage of the world's merchant fleets increased from 137 to 393 million tons gross. This expansion itself shows how the dependence of nations on maritime transport has increased. The merchant vessel has two essential virtues – its great capacity and its low cost per tonne-kilometre – which hold to fundamental physical laws and assure its remaining the prime means of transport for the foreseeable future. The attack and defence of maritime transport will therefore remain at the heart of naval warfare. There are several other traditional maritime commercial assets which date back to the distant past, like fishing boats; but there are also spectacular new forms of exploiting the sea's wealth, such as oil rigs; soon oil and metallic ores will be brought up from great depths; and doubtless the day will come when floating power stations for harnessing the sea's energy, surrounded, perhaps, by biological farms, are 'normal'.

The third stake for naval action obviously consists of the armed forces operating at sea. Such forces would include not just purely naval forces but also, for example, land-based aircraft, which can intervene far out at sea. And everything points to an enormous expansion in the role of space in naval actions — a role that is already important today.

In summary, the role of a naval arm in war, considered on an indefinite time scale, can be broken down as follows:

1 When naval action is brought in direct support of land warfare it can assist with the transport of troops, their landing by force, fire support and heavy logistic support.
2 Naval action can also be purely naval — that is, it can be aimed at other naval elements or it may consist of autonomous operations against shore targets. One of its particular objectives is to seize control of the sea so as to gain freedom of action in its area of operations.
3 All these actions are aimed, at the end of the day, at one or other of three common denominators or stakes — territory, maritime commercial assets or forces.

For naval confrontations at the lower levels of intensity, these different possible roles will influence the choice of action at sea, since operations must be conducted with a view to reaching a favourable position in case of a future war.

3

THE PLACE OF NAVAL OPERATIONS TODAY

In a world where nuclear stalemate and innumerable non-nuclear actions aimed at territorial domination coexist, the possibility of a naval confrontation may well be questioned. The question is relevant at all levels of the intensity ladder, and also concerns all the objectives that governments may seek to achieve by war and for which the conduct of war must, in every situation, be suitably adapted. To try to find an answer, we will return to the classification of confrontations and examine in each case the position of modern naval forces faced with the three principal stakes which have been picked out and which, if won, will meet the objectives of the war with which they are concerned.

For all maritime nations the normal state of low tension improperly called peace requires a certain number of naval ships to be deployed because they must supervise the sea space over which they claim rights, such as an exclusive economic zone. Although it should, in the main, be of an administrative nature, such deployment is not entirely peaceful or neutral because it is necessarily conducted in an area that is more or less international, amidst shipping that is certainly international, and by methods that are almost always military or paramilitary. For those maritime nations which are also nuclear — that is, the major powers — low tension also includes the deployment of deterrent naval elements, the nature of which will be investigated later, but which must be mentioned now since they play a very significant role throughout any increase or escalation of violence; it has already been noted that strikes may be made from the sea at the heart of a continent. A low state of tension also allows the deployment of certain resources intended to ensure, or to prepare the way for, control of the sea — above all, those concerned with gathering intelligence, mounting surveillance operations and exerting political pressure. And, since any government prohibits the destruction of the rival resources of a potential enemy at this stage, one may very well see, and frequently does see, various formations and devices for gaining control of the sea overlapping with one another — a situation that is likely to provoke incidents.

Regrettably, crisis in the world today is continual; and it leads to levels of violence above that of the crisis itself. The word 'crisis' was in the political-strategic vocabulary before nuclear deterrence; and history has known innumerable crises, particularly at sea. The absence of any frontier to separate antagonists who are not in a state of open hostility, and the international character of the high seas, encourage a kind of confrontation which is first and foremost a test of wills. The object is to impress an antagonist by a series of gesticulations without anything worse happening. The resulting pursuits, trailing operations, close encounters and marking of ships, and, indeed, the harassment of naval units as well as commercial interests, are all old customs — just like the discussions and negotiations that they aim to support.

These types of crisis have their own characteristics, which are worth stating:

1 They may accompany numerous conflicts of the kind the world experiences constantly — the Korean war, the Vietnam war, the war in Algeria (despite the absence of naval opposition), the Icelandic 'cod war', radio warfare, piracy, and so forth.
2 They can involve problems of naval air surveillance, deployment, sea keeping and endurance, command and control to an extent and degree of complexity not far removed from those of actual war.
3 They can last a long time — perhaps for several years.
4 They can concern any nation, nuclear or otherwise, and whether or not directly involved in deterrence; but it has to be said, taking account of the balance of deterrent between

the superpowers and the existence of political systems which divide the world, that a crisis today almost always has some background of deterrence.

It is, however, nuclear crisis that will be examined in detail because it is the most serious. By nuclear crisis, we mean a crisis between nuclear nations which are still deterred from declaring war but are already engaged in a process of political confrontation with all the implied demands, denials, back-tracking, putting the armed forces on stand-by, and so on.

Will a crisis between the nuclear powers be of long or short duration? It is clearly impossible to give a plain answer because there are so many political scenarios that can lead to crisis. But the important point is that it *may* be long, for it is reasonable to assume that the leaders in a crisis, conscious of the devastating consequences of a nuclear exchange, will seek to exhaust all other possibilities before resorting to it. If it is short it will result either in a return to so-called peace or in one of the kinds of war that will be looked at later. For the moment, the case of a prolonged crisis will be examined and an attempt made to establish the most relevant features.

First of all, crisis gives rise to intense operational intelligence gathering, since each participant has an urgent need to know where the others are and what they are doing so as to keep watch on them. Search and surveillance methods (satellites, maritime patrol or AEW (Airborne Early Warning) aircraft, D/F (direction finding), fixed acoustic arrays, etc.) are put into full play. To supplement these, ship and submarine sensors are also exploited to the full, as are communications systems and all means of finding out about the situation. These measures all work because at this stage there is no destruction by the enemy.

Secondly, forces need to be ready to carry out any kind of action their governments may order, either to thwart possible initiatives by the enemy or to put pressure on him. This leads to seeking contact with opposing forces or commercial shipping, and to continual manoeuvring to optimize one's position should the situation worsen. This activity results in movements, deployments, replenishments at sea, reliefs, and the establishment of rules of engagement, all of which are exercised in peacetime but which must now, of course, cover a much larger scale of operations. The top priority for a nuclear nation in this situation is to ensure it has freedom of action for its SSBNs (submarines, ballistic-missile, nuclear; it is assumed, for the purposes of this study, that the missiles have nuclear warheads).

Another very serious concern that governments and high commands share will be the question of how far an adversary can be allowed to deploy freely. In this regard, a particularly important aspect for a government faced with a naval crisis is that it may be necessary to consider the movement of troops and military equipment that are of the greatest importance to possible hostilities. What, at this stage, are the solutions that may be proposed to ensure their safety if the enemy has already deployed? Likewise, what is to be done about one's own commercial assets at sea? Should one take protective measures which will reduce their yield, or take the risk of doing nothing about them?

The operations planned for naval forces by their governments will normally be closely co-ordinated with other operations — diplomatic, military and commercial. The naval command will thereby be under some constraint; and that constraint will be made all the more severe because any situation at sea is, by its nature, fleeting and transitory. It is not, however, impossible for the actions in question to escalate as far as a limited and controlled use of fire power at the initiative of one or other of the antagonists. One of the governments may decide to go so far in order to test the enemy's resolve, choosing naval action because the risk is smaller than on land, where the civil population has to be considered; or perhaps distance, errors in communication or simply a nervous reaction by one of the participants may result in an incident.

All this makes clear the absolute necessity for naval forces to have a reliable communications system and an efficient, effective chain of command. It will be seen, at the end of this brief survey, that the principal features of a crisis entail the involvement of practically all that is the essence of naval warfare, with the obvious exception of the final and true test — general combat. That occurs in war itself.

Before we examine the distinction between total and limited war, an important point must be made. From the start of total war the deterrent has failed, so far as its intention of avoiding all hostile action is concerned. None the less, several options still remain open to the nuclear nations, and above all the principals among them, for trying to avoid complete mutual destruction.

It has already been suggested that total war today must by definition be nuclear. The essential facts are that hostilities commence, that the opponents are nuclear powers, and that a nuclear exchange could result. So as to introduce logic into an examination of the complex events which follow, it is convenient to take as guidelines the three major stakes in naval warfare that have already been singled out — territories, commercial assets (mainly merchant ships) and naval forces.

The territory stake can involve the use of missiles (and, for the moment, these are taken to be SSBN missiles), attack aircraft-carriers or landing forces. In most cases, the play for a territorial stake will provoke battles between forces. For example, when the SSBNs prepare to fire their missiles, the enemy will not know exactly where the SSBNs are but he may have a general idea, and so it is quite possible that he will seek to limit their freedom of action. This creates a problem between forces. When the attack aircraft-carriers take up positions for launching raids, enemy forces will generally seek to oppose them there. Here, too, forces are brought up against each other. When landing troops set out, if they arrive at their destination without opposition, the problem becomes one for the land forces; if there is opposition, it becomes an action between one maritime force and another.

As regards the second stake, commercial assets at sea, it has been seen that during a prolonged crisis between nuclear powers the question of safeguarding merchant fleets and other assets or preparing to attack them will have been postulated, but it has not been possible to say what response might be given. Hence it is not known what the situation will be at the start. It is nevertheless very probable that many merchant vessels at sea, which are most important assets anyway, will be carrying part of the land forces, and it is even more probable that at least one of the belligerents will attack the assets of the other. Whether protection for these has been put in train or not during the preceding crisis, it now becomes an urgent matter. One might imagine that it could be achieved in part by shifting the stream of traffic from its normal course, but this response is bound to be countered by the assailants and therefore, here again, battle will be joined between forces.

With regard to the third stake, there will be numerous engagements between forces at sea and, moreover, these may be deliberately sought for their own sake. Some idea can be gained about what may take place by glancing at what is happening on land. When there is a state of total war, in theory all available resources are, or will be, employed, and so there is war on land as well as at sea. Once fighting has begun, the factors which most affect the war at sea are (1) the chronology of the combat, its duration and the rapidity with which it unfolds; and (2) the way in which nuclear weapons are employed — whether nuclear weapons will be used immediately and massively against all targets, or only selectively and progressively after a conventional phase.

It would be convenient to have precise answers to these questions, but that is impossible. We have to be content with a morsel of theory; though slight, it may none the less be sufficient because it enables some possibilities and even probabilities to be discussed. So far as chronology is concerned, the phase of fighting on land could last from several days to several weeks or, indeed, for longer if a degree of caution exists; and so far as the use of nuclear weapons is concerned it is possible that a nuclear exchange might be progressive, either deliberately so, or as a result of steps taken by the antagonists. What will happen at sea? Engagements may take place immediately between the forces which crisis has already brought into contact, after several days for those who were deployed but were not in contact, and a little later for the rest. It is by no means certain that engagements will be nuclear straight away; if they are not the situation will be one of conventional naval warfare but conducted under a nuclear threat which may last for days or weeks. Yet, whether immediately or after a period of conventional warfare, fighting will almost inevitably escalate to nuclear warfare in a total war between people who have nuclear weapons. And it is inevitable that several of the powers involved will have nuclear weapons.

Nuclear battles can occur after various deterrent procedures and can take various forms on the field of action: these will be discussed later with reference to the different aspects of naval warfare. For the moment, however, what concerns us is merely its occurrence, at the initiative of one or other of the belligerents, whether the first nuclear attack takes place on land or at sea.

The way in which a nuclear battle is approached in the final hours will have much influence on its outcome. The battle will be very intense and will last a few hours, a few days, or maybe longer. The dispersion and mobility of naval units, whether belonging to the navy or to the merchant marine, make it impossible to imagine that everything will disappear in a few minutes. There will therefore be a period of intense naval activity involving nuclear tactics. What happens afterwards will either be a restoration, to some extent, of the deterrent principle — which takes everybody back to the original situation, except that there will now be winners and losers among the forces involved; or else a total failure of the deterrent, with nuclear warfare escalating to its extreme limits.

Taking the case where the deterrent has failed and the nuclear exchange is in full swing or has finished, and the destruction on land is immense — what happens now? It is impossible, of course, to prejudge the decisions of governments or the organizations that will have taken their place. But it is reasonable to assume (and the assumption will be justified later) that, by reason of the dispersion and mobility of ships at sea, the nuclear exchanges will leave remnants that are by no means negligible, at least to the 'winner'. It could well be that, even in total war, such remnants could still ensure control of the sea, thus putting into play the strategic possibilities for manoeuvre offered by seaborne transport, the conveyance of supporting facilities, the provision of adequate communications and, in other words, the means of making the final hour decisive.

Perhaps this is the point to pass on to limited war. In the foregoing attempt to classify wars, it was pointed out that a wide variety of 'limited' wars can be imagined. It will be helpful, therefore, to examine the possible types of limited war, in the context of the part naval warfare could play. We might consider whether or not limited war can arise out of total war; whether, in other respects, limited war is possible between nuclear powers, or between non-nuclear powers, or where one power is nuclear but does not use its nuclear weapons.

Limited war could arise from total war if a war that was initially conceived as total became bogged down. This could happen if the first assailant were dissatisfied with the results of his first nuclear attack, or if set procedures for restoring the deterrent were in play, or if internal influences held back a full nuclear exchange; and all of this is possible without there having been a decisive result on land. A period of uncertainty could ensue during which the heads of government would be looking for a solution; in the meantime a state of war could continue with greater or lesser intensity. At sea, sufficient warships and merchant vessels would remain to carry on the fighting, and it is probable that the SSBNs of certain countries would still be carrying at least some of their strategic nuclear missiles.

Passing on to the case of a limited war not arising out of total war but taking place between opposing nuclear powers, it has to be asked how such a war could occur and according to what rules it could be fought. The case is generally thought to be untenable and is usually ruled out by the fact that the great nuclear powers, faced with the prospect of a limited conflict, have so far always avoided a direct confrontation between their own forces — precisely because they fear it would escalate towards the nuclear extremes. However, the case is worth examining all the same in light of the underlying nature and aims of war which have already been discussed. Without trying to evaluate the probability of such an event, one can conceive that an ambitious power, frustrated in its wish to acquire total supremacy because it fears the effect of total war, is nevertheless capable of taking the risk of seeing this happen because it believes its state of readiness is such that it can put the brakes on any escalation and tolerate the damage. Why should such a power not envisage acquiring, at the very least, partial supremacy, while avoiding too much conflict with the vital interests of an enemy? If this is agreed to be feasible in principle, why and how could it arise?

Without claiming to exhaust all the possibilities, we can envisage two possible situations. Firstly, a power might decide to seize a distant territory unprotected by the nuclear deterrent which supplies resources to a potential enemy, partly to acquire the resources for itself and partly to weaken the enemy, and anticipating that, although the venture will be opposed by appropriate forces, it will not result in an escalation to the extremes. Assuming that the enemy reacts, limited warfare would ensue, with a naval component originally intended for naval support of operations on shore. Alternatively, a more or less clandestine attack on commercial shipping at fairly long range might be considered; by regulating the attacks according to the reaction, such action would weaken the enemy while being difficult to counter. The result would be limited naval warfare which would not necessarily lead to the extremes, but could be vicious and prolonged.

Last in the list of possible limited wars is the case of a war between non-nuclear powers or between powers where only one is nuclear. If one of the powers is nuclear it is assumed that nuclear weapons will not be used, because otherwise it would be a special case of total war which would leave little room for naval warfare. The war would therefore be conducted by conventional naval warfare. And, since only one nuclear power is assumed to be entering the lists, and since the powers with any real means of fighting a naval war are chiefly the nuclear powers, it appears that the probability of seeing any considerable naval warfare of this type is relatively low. That is, moreover, why serious and deadly wars like the Korean, Vietnamese and Arab—Israeli conflicts had only quite minor naval participation. However, it is as well to remember that the concept was actually demonstrated during the war between India and Pakistan, which included an authentic naval component; and there are other theoretical possibilities of such a war occurring — around the South American continent, for example.

But there is another possibility which is much less hypothetical: a maritime power might contemplate armed intervention in a distant, 'secondary' conflict which is in some way the result of a great power's indirect strategy. Although history has led us to think that intervention of this kind would not lead to a naval war because the maritime power would not have an enemy at sea, this line of thought should be reconsidered, for the following reasons. Firstly, the winning of independence by many new nations tends to be accompanied by a desire — part rational, part instinctive — to have armed forces, which then proliferate. Secondly, the growing tendency to appropriate the sea's resources or areas of the sea itself impels these new nations to acquire naval forces. Thirdly, modern techniques allow, as will be seen, a hugely destructive weapon potential to be mounted on a small aerial or naval platform, and there are plenty of geographical locations which favour the use of such means; a certain level of naval warfare is thus within reach of even modest budgets. For example, outside NATO and the Warsaw Pact, there were nearly 200 submarines, about 400 fast motor boats armed with missiles and more than 500 fast torpedo boats in the world in 1980. So the type of warlike operations discussed here would encounter more and more opposition at sea, a factor with which the maritime nations will have to reckon.

So far in this account of the different kinds of naval confrontations that could occur in the world today, we have begun with the everyday situation which is called peacetime – often enough a prelude to confrontation – and then described the continuing crisis that accompanies situations of regional tension, which has almost never ceased to exist since 1945, and the serious crisis which could bring the nuclear powers into conflict but does not lead to open war because they are restrained by fear of nuclear retaliation. The various types of war have been briefly examined: total, and therefore nuclear, war; a derivative form arising out of a prolongation of total war; and finally the cases where a war that was from the outset a limited one might involve either nuclear or non-nuclear powers. Although the list may be incomplete, it is substantial enough to provide an adequate basis for answering the question which is the focus of this chapter.

It seems clear that in the world today, with its strategic nuclear balance, its political blocs and its tensions, there is room for naval confrontations to take place. On the other hand, in view of the multiplicity of possible situations and the various types of confrontations that could result, it is impossible to indicate with any certainty what is most likely to happen, although a countless number of different prospects can be imagined. The most likely situations include:

1 Tension, where confrontation is a potential hazard

2 Continuing crisis, represented at sea by a kind of preliminary naval warfare on a limited scale, without a nuclear threat, liable to last for years
3 Serious crisis, represented at sea by highly developed preliminary naval warfare or skirmishing, albeit without actual bloodshed, under a nuclear threat, liable to last for several months and posing gigantic maritime problems as much for merchant shipping as for naval forces
4 A period of open conventional fighting, under a nuclear threat, for or against freedom of action for SSBNs, liable to last for days or weeks
5 A phase of amphibious landing operations with conventional opposition, under a nuclear threat, liable to last for days or weeks
6 A period of fighting between the remnants — the survivors — for control of the sea, with or without the continuance to some degree of a nuclear threat, lasting for an indeterminate period
7 A war far removed from any sanctuaries, whose purpose is to seize territory which is not truly vital, between maritime nuclear powers that do not want to escalate to the extremes
8 A purely naval limited war, for or against commercial assets at sea, between maritime nuclear powers that do not want to escalate to the extremes
9 A classical naval war between non-nuclear powers or possibly between one nuclear power behaving as if it were non-nuclear and a non-nuclear one
10 A distant war between one maritime power and a power with a comparatively small navy with a threat of reaction at sea which is by no means negligible.

It has also to be said that there is no place in the list for the type of war which used to take pride of place — naval warfare on a grand scale, with no holds barred but without any nuclear threat, between major maritime powers. Such a war seems exceedingly unlikely, as will be obvious if the possibilities of naval confrontations are examined closely. Having succeeded to some extent in locating where naval confrontations could in theory occur, we can now embark on some more concrete considerations about them.

Part II

The General Characteristics and Context of Naval Operations

This study has so far attempted to identify the geostrategic circumstances that could lead to naval confrontation. Like the list of possibilities compiled in the last chapter, the list of different types of naval warfare that different circumstances could bring about is rather long. In spite of the diversity of origins and ultimate results, however, naval confrontations will always be characterized at sea by ship movements, searches and engagements, which are the everyday reality, and whose modes, tempo and actual conduct depend, above all, on enduring characteristics peculiar to operations at sea, on the context within which a confrontation develops and on the state of technology and tactics at the time.

This part of the book will examine those permanent characteristics as well as certain aspects of their context in order to establish the conceptual and physical environment in which the direct actors in a naval operation function. It will be seen that the general characteristics of naval action are mainly attributable to the peculiarities of the marine environment and the combatant adapted for it — the warship.

Two groups of non-naval factors, or contextual elements, can be singled out. The first is centred on the important influence on naval warfare of the advent of nuclear weapons. The introduction of nuclear weapons into naval operations brings about a situation entirely different from a simple evolution of weapons systems. The new strategic balances which have been established as a result of the nuclear deterrent rely on a concept of relative forces between states which largely goes beyond naval operations to become, first, one of the contextual elements we are examining here. In addition, besides their principal, deterrent effect, and on account of it, nuclear weapons have secondary effects on other problems such as the conduct of a naval engagement, and they also raise questions such as what can be done about protecting merchant shipping and other assets at sea. The second group of contextual elements comprises the non-military stakes in naval warfare which were defined earlier to serve as parameters for analysis — namely, land territories and commercial interests and assets at sea.

4

GENERAL CHARACTERISTICS OF OPERATIONS

Like land and air environments, the marine environment is a potential theatre for military operations, and the warship is central to these operations. Both the marine environment and the warship have their own characteristics which in turn give naval operations specific features, and two important elements in the marine environment are the geographical and legal aspects.

The most distinctive geographical feature — that which makes the sea so different from the land — is the uniformity of its surface. There are no contours on the sea, no hills and valleys, no built-up areas; there are no road signs (or very few), no frontiers and no single prescribed route. Friends and enemies alike can come and go anywhere as they please. Militarily speaking, this is the key point because it means that one can very rarely reduce a study of an enemy's possible courses of action to a few probabilities. The first operational requirement is to locate the enemy. One may find oneself more or less next door to him, but one is free to deploy where and how one wishes. Another characteristic of the marine environment is that, while it is penetrable by a moving body, it is difficult to detect things moving in it, such as submarines. So far as social geography is concerned, the sea carries the merchandise which, as already noted, is so essential to life throughout the world.

Turning to the legal aspects of the marine environment, these have some very special characteristics of their own. Despite years of diplomatic activity concerning international and national rights at sea, practically nothing had been firmly agreed by 1980. Indeed, legislation is effective only if it is applied universally and if some kind of recognized police force supervises its application. This is by no means always the case at sea; and the efforts required for maintaining surveillance of a 200-mile economic zone mean that the situation is one where only internal and territorial waters are considered as belonging to the bordering state but there is no universal agreement as to their extent, their limits are not marked, there are no customs posts, and there is free right of peaceful passage through them for all. Everywhere else the rules of the high seas apply, with unimpeded passage for all which reinforces the geographical uniformity of the sea. There is no territory to defend and there are no laws any more than there are contours to stop friends and enemies from mixing and elbowing each other at sea. On the other hand, the scarcity of agreed laws and the absence of an omnipresent police force allow conduct that would be held illegal on land — electronic espionage, pirate broadcasting, smuggling of all kinds, pollution, lack of social security for workers, piracy (which is still encountered quite frequently on certain seas) and even the unilateral — albeit more or less discreet — use of force.

These basic legal facts of life have consequences which are sufficiently established to become new factors themselves. The first is that, because the law at sea is so weak, the relative size and relationships of forces at sea play a part even in peacetime; and the best way to mitigate the weakness of the law is to maintain a political presence and establish 'habitual usage' as a valid legal precedent. Secondly, the boundaries between peace, crisis and war are far less clear and much more fluid than they are on land.

The tendency of governments to appropriate tracts of sea, which has developed since the sea itself started to become commercially attractive, gives rise to a considerable risk of creating increased tension if it is not accompanied by true international agreement in defining the limits which the conference on 'the law of the sea' sought to obtain and which governments are supposed to ratify.

The warship is the second characteristic element of naval operations. Operating in the environment for which it is intended, and long considered as a pawn in the military game, it has its own physical and legal characteristics. The warship is, first of all, slow. Its operations are therefore lengthy and it has to start deploying well in advance of the operation for which it is intended. But it also has the capacity to remain on station, thereby exerting political pressure, or simply waiting to do whatever is required. It also has the important attribute of being autonomous: the weapons systems' operators live on board; it is capable, to some extent, of self-maintenance; it always carries its munitions on board and is therefore constantly ready for action. All this makes it a readily manoeuvrable strategic pawn. It is fairly independent of political predicaments in the countries in whose neighbourhood it sails, and it is particularly well suited to showing the flag or to the projection of power (or whatever it might be called) wherever its political masters desire. Its freedom of movement is reinforced by the fact that men-of-war have been seen, for centuries, performing evolutions on seas all around the world and putting in at all the ports: people are used to them.

From a legal point of view, the warship's characteristics accord both with its physical autonomy and with legal administration, such as it is, on the high seas. That is to say, a warship has a large degree of autonomy in this area as well; and the captain represents his country. To illustrate this point, let me quote the relevant paragraph from the regulations for officers in the French navy:

> Officers, who are at one and the same time military officers and men of the sea, represent France at all times on the high seas and, when therein, in foreign territorial waters.
>
> Their task is to look after her interests and to protect her nationals. Commanding officers of ships and naval forces are appointed by order, and holders of these posts receive letters of authority.[1]

At international level, although this special position of warships' commanding officers is perhaps less explicitly laid down than in the written law of France, it none the less exists.

Naval operations have specific characteristics derived from the environment in which they take place and from the military

[1] Décret no. 75—1207, 22 December 1975.

tools they use. These characteristics are a certain continuity between situations of so-called peace, crisis and war, the huge dimensions of space and time and a number of particular constraints.

The geographical and legal uniformity of the sea, the part played by naval 'presence' at sea, the common use of force, the absence of frontiers and the freedom of traffic all give rise to the fact, already noted, that even in peacetime potentially hostile naval forces are everywhere, including regions where one would certainly prefer not to see them. The natural reaction is to keep a watch on them, often at very close quarters. Moreover, there are sometimes good reasons for fearing that unarmed vessels – such as fishing boats, working in contested areas – sailing under their national flag may be intimidated. A foreign warship or an intelligence-gathering auxiliary surprised in territorial waters may have to be told to clear out; or it may be necessary to force an unidentified submarine to the surface by holding contact with it to exhaustion.

This brief survey of the current situation suggests that even in peacetime a certain amount of military force may be used at sea, albeit at the lowest level, that of intimidation. Since there are no frontier posts separating neighbours and making the political situation clear-cut, one must show one's neighbour on the spot that he will not be allowed to use intimidation without a sharp reaction. And it is quite evident that, in a climate of deterrence, this type of conduct is vested with additional importance, for it is a demonstrable and abiding proof of resolution. Further, it is clear that, if political tension arises between governments concerned with actions of this sort, a confrontation that is firm but generally polite in peacetime could easily become more acid, taking the form of deliberate harassment of shipping with opposing forces being replenished at sea and relieved on station, all this being accompanied in the capitals concerned by remonstrations, explanations and other political gambits.

Furthermore, taking account of the possibility that harassment at sea could be progressively increased without too much risk, it is not difficult to imagine that this could be exactly the method chosen by a government to test an enemy's resolve. In any case, if there is no slackening of tension and if war breaks out, naval forces will already be fully occupied with business on their own terrain. This continuity between the different levels of confrontation, this continuing role for navies in making a show of force — not through intelligence services or through journalists acting as intermediaries but directly and visibly between opposing sides — is thus a specific feature of naval operations.

The fact that they cover large dimensions is the second characteristic of naval operations. In fact, even if a naval operation is mounted with only the minimum means, it will take place over a wide area and will probably last for a considerable time. This relates to the point already made about the characteristics of the marine environment and of the warship. Since an enemy can be anywhere and take any route, a warship must always be capable of intercepting him on or in any part of the ocean and therefore be able to travel very far to find him. In naval matters, operational distances are reckoned in hundreds if not thousands of nautical miles. A naval operation can strike at an enemy wherever he is most vulnerable, even if that is distant; and a warship lends itself to this purpose, either alone or as a vector for other forces. Naval operations therefore suit indirect strategy very well, provided that they are planned on a large enough scale.

A naval action is transitory and fleeting. Something obvious has to be remembered here: naval operations involve highly mobile forces, and the situation changes from hour to hour and even from minute to minute. Finally, there are a number of constraints that are peculiar to naval operations. Since geography does not allow them to limit the number of options open to the enemy, any naval engagement is particularly dependent on operational intelligence. Early warning is a costly preliminary to battle, but it is indispensable to a successful engagement. It is impossible to prepare precise operational plans in advance, as one would on land. Moreover, the distance involved in naval operations demands considerable communications facilities and extensive means of mobile logistic support, and it is essential to deploy early to make up for the slow speed of most surface vessels.

In summary, the marine environment, which is uniform and common to all, and the warship, which is slow but sure and capable of remaining at sea for a long time while being strategically autonomous yet representative of its government, together give naval operations certain characteristics. The principal features are continuity between peace, crisis and war, sheer dimension and the transitory aspect of operations as well as a heavy burden of constraints such as intelligence gathering, operational planning, communications, logistic support and deployment. In spite of certain variations, which will be discussed later, these general characteristics remain constant amid the continual evolution and development of warfare at sea.

5

NAVAL WARFARE AND NUCLEAR WEAPONS

Naval warfare nowadays is bound to have a nuclear context. Indeed, scientific and technical advances over the last 40 years have brought innumerable innovations into the naval panoply. Radar, sonar, electronic warfare, operational intelligence processing, missiles, the conquest and use of outer space: these are just some of the innovations that are profoundly changing the methods and procedures of naval engagements. All these new methods of warfare, and others which will be discussed later, are fully integrated into naval combat operations. There is one technological revolution, however, which outstrips naval operations while at the same time modifying them — the advent of nuclear weapons.

The word 'weapon' suggests fighting; but nuclear weapons in the deterrent role, as has frequently been pointed out, are actually intended to *prevent* fighting. They achieve this by a process of globalizing the threat which has nothing specifically naval about it. Ultimately, strategic nuclear weapons, even when embarked, are a part of the political-strategic context much more than they are a direct factor in naval operations. On the other hand, they impose certain constraints and requirements on the latter. It could be said that nuclear weapons form one essential element of the context of naval operations, while being an integral part of them. For that reason, this chapter will examine the role of a navy in nuclear deterrence, and discussion will be confined to cases where both adversaries are nuclear.

Next, the role of less powerful nuclear weapons technically conceived for fighting between forces — tactical weapons —

must be considered. Because these weapons are nuclear and related by nature to deterrent weapons, their possible use poses serious problems of principle which are not purely operational, and thus should be examined as an aspect of the context. This leads, still in the nuclear context, to another important question which is perhaps more political than military. Seaborne commerce plays a still-growing part in the life of nations, but it is clearly becoming more and more vulnerable to attack. Is it conceivable for merchant traffic to be protected by a system of deterrence similar to that which protects the so-called vital interests of nations?

Nuclear deterrence is based on simple logic. Since the appearance of nuclear weapons with their fearsome destructive capability, the feasibility of deterring an aggressor by the threat of reprisals has taken on an entirely new dimension. The usual inputs for weighing up respectively the stakes and the risks that are incurred in any given venture have been turned upside down. An attack by one nuclear power on another can now bring about a response of such magnitude that the first aggressor's territory would be devastated, whatever the devastation he had himself been able to inflict. There could only be losers in a nuclear exchange. Under such conditions, the process of war becomes unprofitable. There is no point in rehearsing here the numerous studies devoted to this question; nor is there any need for a detailed discussion of such matters as the possible attitudes of the strong towards the strong, the strong towards the weak, the weak towards the strong, sufficiency or overkill strategies, strategies directed at civilian populations or at forces only, or deterrence seen either as a happy situation which favours peace or as an unwelcome restraint which puts a brake on certain undertakings.

Keeping strictly to whatever bears directly on naval strategy, however, the following points are relevant to the philosophy and practice of nuclear deterrence:

1 If a potential aggressor is to be 'deterred', he must be certain of receiving a nuclear counter-strike, even if he has endeavoured to disarm his victim by a first strike against his forces.
2 For that, an ability to launch a second strike must be

available; that is, there must be a method of launching nuclear weapons which can survive a first strike. The platform that is best suited to this purpose today is the nuclear-propelled, ballistic-missile-launching submarine (SSBN); this study will explain why such a submarine has this aptitude, which can be guaranteed to last for a long time yet.

3 There must be enough SSBNs to represent a large enough striking potential; their use must be planned and executed in such a way that there is a very high probability of correct systems functioning; and they must be supported by all the naval resources necessary for ensuring that at all times, including a state of war, they have all the freedom of action they need. It is this which bears most heavily on the greater part of a navy's organization, systems, operations and plans.

But this subject is increasingly well known; and it does not seem essential to go deeper into it here. Nevertheless, we ought not to leave the subject of deterrence without observing that an SSBN's capacity to launch a second strike results from two basic factors: the first is the relative impenetrability of a submarine's environment at present; the second is the mobility of an SSBN within its environment so far as the range of its ballistic missiles (ICBMs) allows, well away from any human infrastructure.

Looking to the future, there may come a time, assuredly distant, when there will be techniques that make it possible to neutralize a submarine vehicle as we know it now; but the sea will none the less remain an environment that allows mobility in all directions without any of the restraints imposed by human habitation. It will still provide a vast and open field for new vessels that are technically better adapted to counter the threats which will appear. Furthermore, long-range cruise missiles already offer an alternative to the ballistic missiles now in service.

A less explored yet more controversial subject than the deterrent role of submarine-launched strategic missiles is the use of tactical nuclear weapons at sea. The difficulty here is that not only are there a number of technical uncertainties but there are also fundamental problems concerning the restrictions that most political powers impose on the use of nuclear weapons by their armed forces, resulting in their use being strictly controlled according to whatever doctrine licenses political manoeuvres in relation to military manoeuvres. In order to try to put these problems in perspective, it will be helpful to look first at some practical aspects of nuclear combat at sea. Then we shall consider the implications a common concern for maintaining 'nuclear virginity' could have for the possible use of tactical nuclear weapons. Finally, we shall attempt to analyse the situation where opponents possess tactical nuclear weapons, and have to face up to them in war, so as to discover what effect this situation may have on deterrence itself.

With regard, then, to the practical aspects of using nuclear weapons at sea, these will first be considered in their role as offensive weapons. How could they help an admiral who used them? One single nuclear weapon, even of relatively high destructive power, cannot make an entire squadron disappear in an instant. To simplify in the extreme, the general rule is that one weapon equals one ship (sunk) — which represents a very significant achievement indeed for a single weapon. Moreover, a nuclear warhead increases the radius of destruction for a weapon in proportion to its range and cost. It makes little sense, in fact, to employ high-performance torpedoes or missiles capable of hitting at ranges of tens or even hundreds of nautical miles in order to deliver a modest conventional explosive when the weapon's costs are counted in millions for each one and when the number available is in inverse ratio to the price. This is still partly true even if the weapons are equipped with terminal-homing devices which ensure that they hit, because conventional warheads are not sufficient to destroy most naval targets.

The increased radius of destruction of a nuclear weapon can also compensate for difficulties arising from inexact information about the position of the vessel under attack — especially if this is an attack-type nuclear submarine (SSN). There is therefore considerable interest on all sides in the offensive use of nuclear weapons for combat at sea.

In view of this, what problem does defence pose to a force that comes under a nuclear attack? In point of fact, a warship is relatively resistant to the effects of a nuclear weapon if it has been designed, and kept ready, with proper training for the crew, for nuclear defence — providing, of course, that an explosion is not too close. Indeed, it is structurally designed to withstand the violent effects of bad weather at sea and is constructed in watertight sections. It would not be too difficult to reinforce its resistance to nuclear blast and protect it from fallout. Moreover, the environment in which it operates may well enable it to escape the effects of radioactive fallout altogether: there is plenty of water from the sea for self-wetting, which greatly decreases the effects of contamination, and there is ample space for manoeuvres to avoid predicted fallout areas. These factors suggest that the effects of a nuclear weapon on a naval force might not be too destructive: if there is adequate separation between ships, only a few of them will be within range of immediate destruction, and many others could avoid or at least limit the secondary effects.

The environment itself is significant in a nuclear battle. Clearly, it would be much less of a constraint at sea than on land, above all in Europe where the population is densely packed, primarily because collateral destruction will be almost nil and secondly because such news as is made public about the use of nuclear weapons will be much more restricted than on land.

Finally, a serious problem should be mentioned. In those countries where the political power keeps a tight rein on the use of nuclear weapons, the practicability of using them at sea is beset with difficulties: because of the transitory nature of naval operations it is difficult to link any authorization for the use of a nuclear weapon to a particular target and a particular time to fire; and also because of the level of reliable communications required for the decision making implied by such action.

Thus, from a practical point of view, nuclear engagements at sea seem, at first sight, to be tempting for an offensive operation; dangerous but not impossible to resist when on the defensive; less unacceptable than on land with respect to their effect on the environment; but very difficult to keep under strict political control.

Under these conditions, what is the situation regarding political concern to keep the world in a state of 'nuclear virginity'? This concern is centred on the need to preserve all the deterrent power of the nuclear threat and is based on the fear that the first usage, even at sea, would make the use of nuclear weapons commonplace and lead to dangerous escalation. Those states whose principal aim is to keep the nuclear deterrent intact as a means of preventing war therefore totally reject the idea of allowing the use of nuclear weapons at sea to become familiar, even if only to destroy warships in the vast ocean wastes. On the other hand, one is much less sure of the attitude of a nuclear power which submits only reluctantly to deterrence and is perhaps on the lookout for a breach that could be turned to its advantage, meanwhile providing itself, against any eventuality, with all that is necessary for a nuclear combat at sea. In particular, it is doubtful whether such a power would believe there to be any appreciable risk of the enemy letting loose a strategic riposte because of the destruction of one of its warships by a tactical nuclear weapon.

Even if one is thoroughly committed to the concept of deterrence, it is important to consider what would happen if one of the opponents disregarded any concern for maintaining nuclear virginity. There are, it seems, two entirely different situations. The first is where the opponent who did not wish to see the use of tactical nuclear weapons become casual and commonplace went so far as to deny itself their possession. It would then be at a disadvantage in relation to an enemy that did possess them and would probably submit to total defeat on the battlefield. The strategic deterrent could not in fact be invoked to protect a military force isolated from its own national territory.

The second case, which deserves a rather more thorough examination, concerns two adversaries who both possess tactical nuclear weapons, and where one wishes to preserve the deterrent and the other goes for the tactical advantages of firing first. We see immediately that symmetry between the two sides could engender a kind of local deterrent: if there is a risk of immediate retaliation, nuclear fire may be seen as losing its advantages. This implies, in fact, that a tactical nuclear retaliation has been left as a threat.

Returning to the arguments developed earlier about defence against nuclear weapons at sea, it is clear that a good deal is known about how to cope with nuclear combat: for example, ships can manoeuvre in relation to the wind; and it is possible to remain for long periods at nuclear action stations and to evaluate the situation correctly, despite all the constraints. On the other hand, if when faced with a first strike by the enemy a political power authorizes retaliation, it must obviously do this in such a way that it is fully effective, even if there is a risk of its being tragically late.

As suggested in the first part of this study, a nuclear battle of this kind would have both winners and losers, even if the winners could not hope to achieve victory without loss. And, equally, this consideration would appear to make nuclear combat an important factor in the evolution of the character of naval warfare, whatever may be the doctrine for the use of nuclear weapons of the political power responsible. Its possibility will clearly have a great bearing on decisions at every stage of a crisis. In part III, after studying the development of the forces, we shall return to the role that the possibility of nuclear combat could play in deterrence, and we shall try to suggest what might be the consequences of the various different developments.

Having so far examined the role of navies in nuclear deterrence, nuclear combat at sea, and the respect or non-respect for the notion of nuclear virginity at sea, we shall continue our discussion of the naval consequences of the nuclear factor by asking a question which is a little unusual but which seems to proceed logically from the arguments for the deterrent: could commercial interests — the merchant fleet and other maritime assets — conceivably be protected by deterrence?

It has been seen, with regard to the place of naval warfare, that maritime transport plays an increasing role in the life of the world; and it will be seen later on that, for technical reasons, its vulnerability will similarly go on increasing. It has been predicted that the potential threats to the stream of seaborne transport will also continue to grow. And it is clear that even now commercial shipping is no longer the only asset at sea which might be the target of opposing naval forces. For anyone who wants to attack commercial assets at sea, the range of possibilities is almost too great to choose from; but for anyone who wants to defend them, the problem is exceedingly difficult (the problems of conventional defence will be discussed in chapter 11). We are used to thinking of deterrence in terms of protecting national territory only, since it seems unlikely that anyone would risk millions of deaths for the sake of a few cargo ships. But in fact, official doctrine associates deterrence more precisely with so-called vital interests. And is maritime transport, for most nations which draw their energy, raw materials and some of their food supplies from overseas, not indeed a matter which is truly vital? Everyday speech would doubtless quite easily assign the epithet 'vital' to maritime transport, but does this stand up to close examination? 'Vital' applies to things which, if done away with, bring about death. In general, nuclear nations dependent on maritime transport possess stocks of the most vital products, and, as long as these stocks are not used up, an interruption to the flow of transport would not be immediately fatal. Thus the time factor is important if a threat of nuclear attack on commercial shipping is to be credible.

On the other hand, how exactly can death be defined for a nation? One could expound at length on this subject, but to show that there is no simple answer it may be enough just to ask the question. Regarding the interruption of maritime transport, one could as well remark that if very severe rationing were introduced by the threatened nation it could maintain essential supplies for a while and thus prolong the time of survival for the country concerned. From that situation, can one go so far as to imagine that when this possibility is exhausted, faced with obvious and imminent danger, a political power could brandish the threat of nuclear reprisals and make the enemy take it seriously? It would be rash to answer such a question in the quiet of an office in peacetime, when clearly the main thing would be the country's resolution and will to defend itself rather than any quantifiable factors.

In the event of a positive response to the question, one comes up against the difficulty of identifying the aggressor, since his method of attack would probably be by submarine. Technically, the difficulties are fairly obvious. However, it would seem that, faced with a major attack of the sort conjectured, the problems would not be insurmountable. Firstly, one can reasonably hope to amass, over a period, positive elements of identification — for example, by forcing a diesel submarine to surface — or at least a revealing concentration of indications about its identity; and, in extreme circumstances, it is conceivable that in such a situation absolute proof might be dispensed with.

To sum up, the advent of nuclear weapons brings about a real transformation in the strategic role of first-rank navies. It has indeed given them the ability to strike directly at the heart of an enemy territory, including a second-strike capability. This ability should be viewed in two ways: on the one hand it involves very heavy operational commitments for the naval command, and that will be reviewed in the following chapters; on the other hand it associates naval tactics with strategic considerations which override them and give them a context which must never be overlooked. Nuclear weapons may also radically change the character of fighting at sea between forces. But the fighting itself is strictly dependent on the strategic context. That, without question, is of major importance. We shall be returning to its role in deterrence when we have examined all the naval developments in progress. Finally, we have asked (without drawing any conclusion) whether it is possible to use a strategic nuclear threat for the purpose of preventing a maritime transport system from being wiped out, if an outbreak of war against commerce had brought a nuclear nation close to the danger of suffocating to death.

6

TERRITORIES, COMMERCIAL ASSETS AT SEA AND NAVAL WARFARE

The advent of nuclear weapons puts naval operations in a strategic context that affects their very concept. The second group of contextual elements to be examined here concerns the physical factors in which the non-military stakes in naval warfare consist — that is, territories and commercial assets at sea. The last few decades have brought about important developments here, and naval thinking must take account of them.

With regard to the possession of land — which is, of course, one of the main foundations of all states — numerous countries have undergone major transformations in the past 35 years. It is not intended fully to examine these here, although in some respects any change in things that have to be defended will influence the type of defence and hence strategic thinking. We shall be content with the more modest aim of pointing out some aspects that concern naval warfare quite closely.

The phenomenon of urbanization, which has been widespread in the developed countries comprising most of the great maritime and nuclear nations, has introduced a vulnerability that a purely rural civilization does not experience: it offers choice targets to anti-city strategies of deterrence. Urbanization is accompanied by a change in the population, which thus becomes more technical, less simple-minded and less accustomed to physical effort than a rural population. Such a population is naturally drawn towards technical solutions for its defence, rather than towards mass guerrilla-style solutions. This is seen as a lasting guarantee for the deterrent strategy. Further, the countries we are most directly concerned with — above all, those belonging to the West — base their expansion on vigorous international trading. They are therefore heavily dependent on the latter, and hence dependent on maritime transport. In addition, this results in an expansion of industrial complexes along the coast and urban concentrations near the sea — and hence within reach of seaborne military operations.

There have been major changes in a traditionally important territorial factor in naval warfare — naval bases overseas which have been depleted along with the general phenomenon of decolonization. This depletion is, however, compensated for to some degree by seeking 'facilities' in foreign ports.

Merchant vessels, in particular among maritime commercial assets, have developed considerably during the past 35 years. The first phenomenon to note is the increase in size of both liquid- and solid-bulk transporters. The average tonnage of tankers throughout the world was, on 30 June 1979, 47,000 tonnes fully laden. And yet these ships have seen only a small increase in speed, which remains generally less than 20 knots. Ships like these are the perfect quarry: they are easy targets to reach and attack; and a huge capital interest is concentrated in a single objective. Moreover, at numerous points of the globe, their draught restricts their freedom to manoeuvre. Here, then, is a development which facilitates attack and seriously complicates defence.

Another important phenomenon is the expansion of containerization for a wide variety of merchandise. It is relevant to naval warfare because it is accompanied by an increase in the speed of the ships concerned which in itself offers possibilities for defence. Containerization can also facilitate the installation of certain defence measures on board — such as containerized helicopters and Ikana ASW missile torpedoes. Finally, there is now a relatively large number of drive-on/drive-off ferries in the world's merchant fleets. Since they can load and unload their cargoes quickly, they would be good auxiliaries for certain military operations.

From this diversification of maritime transport methods it appears that the most serious strategic consideration is still the increasing vulnerability of oil tankers. In addition, exploitation of the sea's resources presents a problem which is altogether new, for example with oil rigs. The equipment is fragile and its weakness is susceptible to particularly troublesome consequences owing to the fact that the exploitation in question is most often to do with a dangerous product such as oil. Here, too, one is faced with a vulnerable target that is easy to attack and difficult to defend. It must therefore be borne in mind that any increased economic vulnerability of a state in respect of its maritime transport and its exploitation of the sea is made more critical by an increase in the military vulnerability of these assets.

While naval operations still possess the reasonably stable foundation constituted by the general environmental characteristics, the context in which they might take place has undergone radical changes. The most spectacular is the direct integration of the naval factor into the global strategic balance-of-power game, which alters the very concept of most major naval operations, over and above changes in material aspects (which will be discussed later). But the physical realities of the context have also developed along with the changes undergone by the passive participants in the naval game — territories and commercial interests at sea.

Part III

Development of the Forces and Naval Strategy

Having set the scene for naval confrontations by talking about their general characteristics, the conceptual influence of nuclear weapons and the changes in the non-military stakes of naval operations, we come to the participants themselves — that is, the naval forces.

Technological developments during the past 35 years have brought about major changes. Radar, sonar, passive listening equipment, electronic warfare in all its forms, data processing, propulsion, guidance systems, telecommunications and other advances have invaded ships and aircraft. And, up above them, space is becoming populated by devices whose military significance is growing rapidly. There is, in fact, an explosion of military and naval technology paralleling that which has occurred in every field today. Although it is not easy to take an overall view of this expansion, it is necessary to do so in order to try to discover the likely effect of these developments on naval strategy. To this end, we shall try to take stock of the changes undergone by the participants in naval operations over the past 35 years by first tracing the logical stages of a naval operation by examining the means by which the various necessary functions are fulfilled; and secondly reviewing the various classical actors themselves — ships, aircraft and so on — so as to see what they have become and what they could become in future. It should then be possible to deduce the consequences for naval strategy.

7

DEVELOPMENT OF THE PARTICIPANTS IN NAVAL WARFARE

As we saw earlier, a naval operation, taken in the broad sense, begins at the stage where the opponents are more or less ignorant of their relative positions. Whoever takes the offensive will be anxious to keep his initial strategic moves secret so as to retain freedom of action and, if possible, achieve surprise when the time for action comes. The defender is equally anxious to locate the enemy, or at least find out roughly where he is, as soon as possible, and to gauge his intentions. Stage one is over when the mutually unknown quantities are revealed. Stage two in the scheme of things consists of preparing for ultimate action: the enemy must be precisely located and all necessary steps must be taken in preparation for action. The third and last stage is that of action itself; and the ultimate and most significant event in any operation is, of course, battle.

Starting, then, at stage one, the strategic approach phase could last for months. In the past, the means of search were eyesight and information picked up from merchant vessels met by chance. Consequently there were frequent cases of total strategic surprise. During the First World War the medium of search on board ship was invariably the human eye. Then wireless telegraphy made its appearance, and strategic information — intelligence — could start to be disseminated rapidly. In the Second World War two very effective new means of search came into general use: the maritime-patrol aircraft, with its large radius of action, extensive optical range and radar; and radio direction finding (DF). Today, direct optical detection is still preferred because it conveys an unequalled wealth of information; the performance of aircraft and their means of detection have increased enormously; and DF over a very wide frequency range has greatly improved. Two newcomers of considerable stature have also made their appearance — the 'spy', alias surveillance or reconnaissance, satellite; and the fixed underwater ground acoustic array.

The naval surveillance satellite is still in its infancy. However, its possibilities are already remarkable: it can, once launched, maintain its orbit for months and carry out a continuous and progressive sweep over the sea areas assigned. However, it still has many limitations: it does not gather and relay information continuously; its ability to identify is probably poor; its certainty of functioning correctly is not 100 per cent; and its manoeuvrability in orbit is either nil or very costly. Meanwhile, such as it is, a 'spy' satellite certainly makes it impossible to keep secret the deployment of a naval force comprised of large surface vessels for more than a few hours, as a rule. This, by itself, is a revolution.

Tomorrow, the great nations who wish to pay the price could probably have at their disposal much more complete systems that were much better fitted for identifying contacts and transmitting continuous information. Then strategic discretion would be a thing of the past; secret deployment over the sea's surface would be impossible. However, it might still be possible to mislead and confuse an observer about the information he receives.

A parallel development is that of fixed acoustic ground arrays for detecting submarines which, for the moment, escape detection by reconnaissance satellites, but their prospects are far from being as sure as those of satellites. The sounds they pick up are extremely difficult to classify. An enemy submarine can also escape detection altogether by not making any detectable noise, albeit at the cost of reducing its freedom of action. Moreover, these arrays, whose real performance is still uncertain, cannot be as ubiquitous as satellites; they are expensive; they are subject to serious search restrictions; they take a long time to place in position; they are practicable only in certain limited areas; and they are to some extent vulnerable. Nevertheless, their presence, or even their suspected presence, imposes limitations on the enemy's strategic moves. One feature that reconnaissance satellites and listening arrays have in common is that both are exceedingly expensive and difficult to put into effect. Consequently they are not available to most navies — although all are deeply interested in them.

These new search facilities are not the only important new matters bearing on strategic mobility. Another is that fleets today enjoy considerably more technical autonomy. This is due to the advent of nuclear propulsion and the development of better logistic support at sea.

Nuclear propulsion frees ships from the continual need to refuel at sea because the life of a reactor is at least as long as the interval between major refits. This is especially important for large ships, particularly aircraft-carriers, because they are heavy consumers of fuel, and (for reasons that will be discussed later) for submarines too. Medium-sized surface vessels could also benefit from this type of propulsion; but small ships are not yet considered for this because of technical obstacles preventing nuclear power plants from being installed in small machinery compartments.

With regard to logistic support at sea, the possibilities have been greatly improved and expanded. Liquids and solids can now be much more rapidly transferred at sea during replenishment operations whose time has been reduced from several hours to a few minutes with automatic tensioning, automatic load handling, instant connectors and cargo-carrying helicopters. Diversification has resulted from the greater range of transferable materials and increased facilities for undertaking light repair work at sea thanks to specialized support vessels equipped with stabilizers.

All this gives a well-maintained naval force the ability to remain at sea for several months if necessary, which in turn makes possible strategic moves and groupings that would once have been inconceivable — such as the ability to remain on station — and mitigates the effect of diminishing overseas shore facilities noted earlier. Thus the strategic approach phase is marked by two very important new features: possibilities for methods of search have considerably increased and so has the self-sufficiency of forces at sea.

In the second phase of naval operations, the forces involved will be preparing themselves for ultimate action. At the point where this stage begins, it is assumed that at least one of the opponents has some operational intelligence about the other. More precise information is now needed about the situation in the prospective area of action. What vessels are present in the area? What type are they? Are they friendly, neutral or enemy? How are they formed up? What are they doing? What might their intentions be? It is then necessary to detect, locate, identify and analyse the behaviour of the contacts in order to establish a complete pattern of tactical data. Certain search methods employed during the first phase — for example, maritime-patrol aircraft — can continue to be used. And, of course, ship-mounted sensors in all the units involved will also be put to use. These sensors have advanced steadily since the Second World War but it has to be admitted that their progress has been slow.

Looking now at the principal sensors, we shall first consider those that work above the surface, beginning with radar. Radar achieved its theoretical maximum range early on, in terms of accessibility of the target (i.e. within the radar horizon), the power emitted and wavelengths used. However, spectacular improvements in data rate have been made, to the point where the functions of search, target designation and tracking are integrated; it is now possible to deal with several targets and several weapons simultaneously if the equipment includes electronic scanning (a technique still not in general use). There have also been improvements in discrimination — the ability to cope with interference, whether due to natural causes or caused by the enemy (e.g. Chaff) — and in making radar transmissions rather more difficult to detect. In addition, radar equipment has become more reliable and much less heavy, so that it is now possible to equip even small aircraft with effective radar sets. Despite all these improvements, however, the use of radar must still, strictly speaking, be considered as imprudent unless the risk of revealing one's presence is acceptable.

On the other side of the coin, the passive detection of transmissions over a wider and wider waveband has itself made great progress, from radio frequencies to optical frequencies, including radar and thermal emissions. These are significant innovations. Passive detection methods are themselves undetectable but they are, of course, dependent on the enemy making detectable transmissions. During this stage of operations, passive detection methods may be inadequate. In any case the command will have to choose between the passive detection of enemy transmissions and the use of active methods of detection which are themselves detectable but more reliable. Passive detection can, of course, be enhanced by DF, and by analysis and interpretation (with the aid of intelligence data) with equipment now widely available.

All these sensors, to which must be added the irreplaceable human eye-brain combination, can be carried by ships or aircraft. The shipborne helicopter, which can now be embarked on board vessels, not necessarily naval, of medium or small tonnage, also belongs among the innovations of the last decade in detection and identification at sea, since quite humble vessels can now combine the permanence and stability of a ship with the visual range and speed of an aircraft — a combination which was formerly the preserve of those aristocrats, the aircraft-carriers.

We now turn to the 'silent world' below the surface, where electromagnetic waves can barely penetrate. Here, as above the surface, slow but steady changes are taking place in the field of sensors, and these will be enlarged upon later in connection with submarines. Briefly, although sonar has made great strides, it still offers almost no chance of detecting a submarine that wants to avoid it; passive listening is making headway largely against noisy submarines; while magnetic-anomaly detection equipment (MAD), also improving, is able to relocate an enemy only at very short range.

All these sensors raise, by their very abundance, problems of management: it is not always easy to exploit them to the full (as will be seen later). But they allow the force whose progress we are following through the various phases of its operations to prepare for action with information that can on occasion be remarkably complete and accurate.

The final phase of the operations is battle. At this stage the sensors continue their work in much the same way as before, but the weapons must now go into action.

Traditional arms — guns, torpedoes, ahead-throwing anti-submarine weapons — have all been the subject of continual improvement. Modern gunnery control methods using computers have given fresh life to gunnery by making it considerably more accurate and greatly increasing the speed with which guns can be brought into action — action that can be entirely automatic from first detection to cease-fire. Multi-barrel small-calibre guns with a very high rate of fire and heavy shells are promising new types of traditional gunnery for small, close-range targets. In association with modern radar, both could effectively engage certain types of missiles, even at very short notice. Torpedoes are also making considerable headway in all respects — speed, range, undetectability and acoustic homing. They have the great advantage of hitting underwater; they strike the most sensitive area of a target, whose first need, after all, is to stay afloat, and they benefit from the tamping effect of the sea itself which increases the effect of an explosion underwater. Ahead-throwing anti-submarine weapons (mainly rockets) are giving ground to torpedoes but are still attractive by reason of their comparatively low cost, their suitability for small ships and their improved range.

These advances in traditional weapons are important and in many cases allow them to keep a place alongside their more modern counterparts. But they do not constitute a spectacular breakthrough. The breakthrough is elsewhere; and it is due to entirely new weapons. Missiles are obviously at the top of the list. Having made their début at the end of the Second World War, they now play a pervasive role in the panoply of armaments — at sea perhaps more than anywhere else. Missiles are the strategic weapon *par excellence*. Always evolving, they will soon attain a range of 6,000 nautical miles and could have perhaps seven independently manoeuvrable nuclear warheads per missile. A missile of this kind will be able to reach any target from the most widely scattered launching sites, and with a very high probability of penetration. Even with a lower level of performance, it will enable an SSBN to strike at the heart of a continent. We shall return to the subject of submarine-launched missiles and the revolution they have brought about in the strategic potential of navies.

At the tactical level, the many kinds of missiles in service have to be distinguished by their purpose. Surface-to-surface missiles are now so light, easy to use and efficient that virtually any ship, and, most significantly, a small ship, can now carry a destructive power greater than that of gunnery. This phenomenon has wide implications, which we shall discuss later.

Progress in surface-to-surface missiles consists in seeking as low a flight-profile as possible so as to delay detection, improving the warheads, seeking the best position for exploding a warhead by means of a steep dive at the end of the trajectory and, finally, increasing the range. So far as the last point is concerned, the problem is how to guide the missile when the target is beyond guidance range of the launcher. One way of doing this is for the launcher to relay guidance commands via some other intermediary that can locate the target and guide the missile — for example, another ship, an aircraft or a satellite. Another method is for the missile itself to have the capacity to locate and identify. In the absence of operational experience, little is known about how the principal navies stand in this respect. But the combination of greatly increased range, which is known to have been achieved for several missile types (of which one is the so-called cruise missile), improvements in course direction (whether autonomous or not), the ability of missiles to locate and identify — and components for all these improvements are available at least in the major countries — makes missiles today one of the great factors dictating the future of naval warfare. Indeed, if the aircraft-carrier dethroned the armoured ship because it was capable of striking the enemy while itself remaining protected from attack, a high-performance missile could in the long term threaten the aircraft-carrier because it matches its reach while having a much less vulnerable launching platform (in extreme circumstances this could be on land) and the weapon system is far simpler to operate.

Before leaving the surface-to-surface missile, we should recall the problem caused by its being equipped with a nuclear warhead, which has already been raised with regard to nuclear warfare at sea. It should also be noted that, in addition to conventional-explosive warheads and nuclear warheads, new explosives or charges with a chemical content are certainly possible.

Various types of missiles in use against aircraft have radically changed the nature of fighting between ships and aircraft. In some instances, an attacking aircraft can be engaged even before it has a clear view of the situation itself — and with a high chance of hitting. However, with conventional radar where data rate is limited, the number of targets that can be engaged simultaneously is low; and consequently the defences can be saturated if an attacker is prepared to pay the price.

With a purpose-built weapon system, equipped with modern scanning radar capable of dealing with several enemy targets and guiding a number of missiles simultaneously, the situation is entirely different. Faced with the threat of effective reaction from the ship under attack, whether or not it has a high-performance anti-aircraft missile system, an assailant is likely to stand off and launch an air-to-surface missile himself. We have seen that surface vessels will adopt comparable tactics. And submarines too (as will be shown) are beginning to launch missiles, which change their environment from sub-surface to surface flight, against surface ships. Since missiles from three different sources can thus be directed against surface vessels, anti-missile defence has become a key issue for surface vessels. Solutions, or projected solutions, abound. The conventional gun, brought up to date with multi-barrel rapid fire, is, as we have suggested, not yet obsolete, provided it is accompanied by an adequate detection system and sophisticated fire control. The anti-missile missile has already proved its worth, and we shall certainly see great advances in this field, especially in association with modern scanning radar which alone is capable of providing the necessary data rate.

So far as new weapon systems are concerned, one must include all the possibilities of active electronic warfare — that is to say, the whole array of decoys and jammers which, while not killers in themselves, are handled rather like weapons. This is obviously an expanding area where secrecy, surprise and cunning are paramount. Blinding enemy sensors with false targets or transmissions that saturate the frequencies, presenting the incoming missiles with baits on which they will home more readily than their genuine targets — these are all methods of destroying the effectiveness of enemy homing missile systems. From this stems the need for opposing all these counter-measures by counter-counter-measures which may be either of the same kind themselves (where it is mainly a question of changing frequencies at the right moment) or, more radically, a change to a totally different system enabling detection, guidance and terminal homing to be effected without transmitting by using instead the various enemy emissions of radar, infra-red, thermal or light rays.

Looking to the future, some entirely new weapons could appear quite soon. For example, there are the so-called neutron gun and the laser weapon which could eventually become the anti-missile weapons for large ships. Although the latter is immensely heavy and very unreliable in the experimental forms being tested by the superpowers today, such a weapon, if it became operational, would have the exceptional advantage of providing a virtually limitless supply of zero-time 'projectiles'.

Weapons of war at sea have thus undergone spectacular developments which will doubtless continue. The variety of missiles that can be adapted to all conceivable types of attack, and the variety of electronic warfare methods capable of being used in conjunction with them, give naval engagements, even today, an entirely new appearance. In the future they could advance still further if they become more intelligent. In time there may be weapons without projectiles which could give big ships something like the 'death ray' of science fiction.

At the end of this examination of technical developments, seen through the principal phases of a naval operation, some factors that are common to all stages must be emphasized. The broad range of means available, the enormous distances that separate some of the actors, the often very short time between detection and attack, and the number of reactions that have to be triggered make it impossible to exercise command without both a very reliable, high-capacity communication system and effective methods of processing the information received. The answer lies in telecommunication satellites and operational data processing.

The logical thread we have tried to follow in unravelling naval operations — reduced for the purposes of this study to a simple outline — has guided this preliminary examination of the development of a naval force's methods and resources. It might now be useful to re-examine this development in a perhaps more familiar way by considering one by one the traditional actors in a naval engagement — submarines, aircraft-carriers, traditional surface warships, conventional mine-warfare units and naval aircraft.

This second survey of the material factors characterizing

naval forces will begin with submarines and everything connected with them — their enemies and the various kinds of confrontation. The methods of fighting between submarines and their adversaries never cease to grow in scale and complexity, and enormous advances are being made in the design of submarines themselves.

During the Second World War, the German U-boats were only beaten by a combination of ships and aircraft which were able to restrict their freedom of action and engage them at every stage of their short lives — when under construction, in transit, on patrol and sometimes only after they had carried out their attacks. Today the range of methods for achieving a combination of this sort is expanding and tomorrow it will assume enormous proportions. We shall attempt to set the scene before considering the future of war beneath the surface.

The development of submarines as weapon carriers has been great, the prime factor here being the advent of nuclear propulsion. The submarine benefits more than any other vessel from this, since it is thereby freed from the constraint of having to feed its propulsion machinery with air; without the problems of refuelling, the submarine acquires technical autonomy, and the length of time it can spend at sea is limited only by the crew's endurance and by maintenance requirements.

The SSN (nuclear-propelled attack-class submarine) and the SSBN are therefore true submarines. Moreover, they have huge reserves of power, and have become as fast as and often faster than surface ships; this has revolutionized not only their capacity for strategic mobility but the whole concept of submarine warfare. Technological progress has also enabled submarines to dive to several hundred metres and thus to be much more mobile in the third dimension than they used to be. Finally, submarines are making headway in noise reduction, the extreme military importance of which will be seen later. However, the technology involved in all this is expensive and the secrets are well guarded.

A weapon carrier must, of course, have sensors. Still mainly centred on acoustics, a submarine's sensors have not undergone as spectacular a transformation as has the vehicle itself, but they have still benefited from the advances in this field pointed out earlier, and the utilization of data received has improved so much that new perspectives have been opened. Advances in detection are due principally to better signal processing, to a more refined knowledge of sound propagation (allied to the submarine's greater vertical mobility which allows it to listen at the optimum depth) and to new types of very low-frequency passive sonar equipment using towed arrays. Submarine sonar capabilities are also being improved through the development of sound analysis and classification with the aid of computers. However, there is also a large gap between the top of the scale, represented by the ability to detect other submarines, and the lower end of the scale.

In order for a submarine equipped with sensors to be a fighter, it must also have weapons. For a long time, submarines have suffered from a very real weakness: the range of their weapons has always been far less than the means of detection. Weapons that change their environment (sub-surface to surface) have entirely altered this state of affairs. We have already referred to the revolution brought about by strategic missiles. At the tactical level, the weapons that pass from one medium to another are SUBROC, SS-N-15 and SS-N-16, and SM 39 whose ranges are reckoned, or will be reckoned, in tens of nautical miles. This, together with nuclear propulsion, is without doubt the most revolutionary new factor affecting submarine weapons: it restores the strategic role to submarine fleets and it makes many proven anti-submarine tactics out of date. But it also introduces a new element differentiating the countries that can afford such expensive weapon systems in SSBNs or high-performance SSNs from those that cannot. Yet, although a nuclear submarine is freed from the need for air and is no longer restricted to eyeball-to-eyeball engagements, it has still not overcome a number of other weighty military constraints: the vulnerability of its hull; the difficulty it has in co-operating with other actors by reason of communication problems which are being resolved only slowly and at a great cost; the continuing inferiority of its means of assimilating the tactical situation from the point of view of interpretation, classification and identification by comparison with direct vision; and also its unsuitability for an overt demonstration of force.

In view of the remarkable advances made by the submarine, how has defence against it developed? Since a submarine's basic characteristic is concealment, its enemies need first of all to find it. We shall start, therefore, with anti-submarine detection methods, then turn to anti-submarine vehicles, looking particularly at their ability to operate the various means of detection, and end with a review of anti-submarine weapons.

First of all, a diesel-powered submarine is obviously liable to detection by radar and visual sighting whenever it has to raise a mast above the water to snorkel — either in transit or when recharging its batteries, or simply to refresh the air for breathing — or when using a periscope or radar mast or when transmitting a signal with a periscopic aerial. Conventional means of detection, therefore, are still valid where an enemy is operating diesel-electric submarines — and such submarines still have a future. But the most important question is how to detect a submarine that remains totally submerged; and it is developments in this area that deserve most attention.

So far as being detected is concerned, a submerged submarine has two physical properties — and only two. These are its magnetic field and, more important, the sound waves it emits or reflects. So far as can be seen, there are no other physical phenomena that could be exploited in the medium term. Having said that, we can briefly discuss the exploitation of the magnetic anomaly set up by a submarine. This procedure has been the subject of considerable advances and will probably progress further still; but its range will never go beyond the requirements of classification, tracking and attacking a submarine that has first been detected by other means. Though limited, this means of relocation is important enough to necessitate the parallel development of demagnetization and greater diving depths for submarines.

However, it is the multiple forms that acoustic detection is assuming today that require more careful consideration. There is no spectacular scientific or technological breakthrough here; but dogged efforts in this field over many years, in particular by the United States navy, are gradually bearing fruit. Active sonar is being improved, specialized and diversified. Convergence-zone and bottom-bounce and deep-towed sonars, all at low frequency, can achieve ranges in the order of tens of thousands of metres. Passive listening at very low frequencies has undergone substantial developments, though in fact not much is publicly known yet about its operational effectiveness. In the meantime it is certain that the United States navy is giving it high priority, with regard both to towed arrays for surface ships and submarines and to fixed ground arrays capable of making an initial detection of noisy submarines over wide areas. These types of detection are inseparable from a thorough knowledge of the sound spectrum of those vessels which have to be detected and from effective ways of analysing and classifying the detections made.

Low-frequency sonic detection methods have already accelerated the race for silencing submarines, and it is probable that they will lead to a kind of 'acoustic warfare' related to 'electronic warfare' — a complex game of active and passive counter-measures and counter-counter-measures. It should be pointed out that in the race for silence a conventional modern submarine on electric motors is well placed. In the future, then, vast schemes may be planned for methods of eventually breaching, in certain specially instrumented sea areas, the former undetectability of submarines — or at least those that are noisy either because of their construction or through some tactical error. Needless to say such complexes, if they ever see the light of day, will cost a truly formidable amount in terms both of technical effort and of money.

There are several kinds of platform carrying some means or other of anti-submarine detection equipment. Among these, the aircraft has the advantage of speed and an incomparable breadth of both radar and optical coverage, as well as being able to carry magnetic-anomaly detection equipment (MAD); but it is penalized by being entirely unconnected with the water and having access to acoustic information only through the intermediary of sonobuoys, which are expensive and have a necessarily limited life and capability.

The surface ship, riding horseback on the air—sea interface, enjoys both the advantages and the disadvantages of its situation. Partly in air, it benefits from radio links which are convenient for communicating with other actors in the anti-submarine battle, and from 'natural' living conditions for its crew; partly underwater, it has access to the marine environment that carries acoustic information, but this access is not optimal because the instability of the sea surface and a ship's shallow draught make it difficult to offer ambient silence to its sonar and force it to adopt cumbersome and complicated towing arrangements to select the best depth for sonic detection equipment.

A relative newcomer to ASW is the helicopter, which today is a good vehicle for carrying sonar because, while it is hovering, it can 'dunk' a transducer without movement relative to the water and hence place it in good acoustic conditions. But its useful payload is fairly limited, and this prevents it from carrying very large sonar sets; however that may be, it is flourishing on board numerous ASW ships of medium or large tonnage. It also has the great merit of being suitable for embarkation on a merchant ship which can speedily be equipped to receive it.

Amongst all the ASW detection platforms, the submarine itself has advanced most notably. Indeed, when its enemy is continuously submerged and is only vulnerable to initial detection by acoustic means, it is well placed to effect this in optimal conditions because it is perfectly integrated with the sound-carrying medium. However, an anti-submarine submarine needs sophisticated equipment and must be very quiet. Submarine-versus-submarine warfare is a battle of performance and skill between the hunter and the hunted; and the victor will be the one who makes the best of his abilities.

Finally, regarding fixed acoustic sensors, the idea of a vehicle is replaced by that of a fixed acoustic array or grid laid on the seabed. The positions and methods of using ground arrays are, of course, kept secret.

With regard to anti-submarine weapons, the panoply today includes ahead-throwing weapons, increasingly sophisticated torpedoes launched by submarines, surface ships or aircraft; and medium-changing missiles. To these must be added the immobile ASW threat constituted by mines, which have also been improved, and their more complex relatives like the American Captor which releases a torpedo when a submarine passes by.

One notable innovation, of course, presents a problem already frequently mentioned here: whether nuclear warheads, fitted to the ASW weapons of certain countries, will be used as a general practice.

Combatants in submarine and anti-submarine warfare — undersea warfare as it can generically be called — are, today, very different from what they were during the last conflict when serious undersea warfare took place — the Second World War. No significant ASW lessons have been learned from any of the colonial or minor wars that have taken place since. The present era is, however, affording maritime nations some experience — albeit necessarily limited — of the problems of ASW detection because, quite apart from operational exercises, we are living in a time of permanent tension at sea: SSBNs are constantly on patrol and every opportunity is taken to track unidentified submarines. Nevertheless there is good reason for considering very carefully the form an underwater war could take today or tomorrow. To assist such speculation, it is best to start with the three naval warfare stakes noted earlier: territories, commercial assets at sea and naval forces.

So far as an attack on national territory is concerned, it has already been noted that submarines armed with strategic missiles are now able to launch strikes at the heart of an enemy state. Enemy defences would probably be aimed either at the missiles themselves or at the launching submarines. With regard to anti-missile defence, all that can be said is that no way can be foreseen, in the medium term, of preventing strategic missiles from penetrating defences if the missiles are correctly fitted with up-to-date equipment and are sufficiently numerous. But what of the SSBN's vulnerability to opposition from the enemy? The answer lies in the nature of a modern nuclear submarine's capabilities, already reviewed, and the characteristics of a deterrent patrol. The latter is a static mission whereby the submarine lies in wait, hidden, to avoid all risks. It keeps quiet and is thereby protected from passive detection. If its missiles have the necessary range, its possible patrol zones are so extensive that the chances of finding an SSBN by active detection methods are practically nil, and the same is true of the zones themselves. Its only periods of relative vulnerability are when sailing from and returning to harbour when its freedom of action is restricted. That is why precautions have to be taken at these critical points in its patrol cycle.

Today, therefore, the submarine seems to be easily the winner in its strategic mission against enemy national territory.

However, its situation in the future must clearly be questioned. It has already been suggested that if, in the long term, a submarine's enemies become sufficiently numerous and if they co-operate with one another and have high-performance ASW equipment, the submarine could have problems at least in stationary or moving patrol zones where comprehensive ASW systems have been established. This suggests that the security of an SSBN on patrol would depend very much on the range of its missiles. With a range of 6000 nautical miles the greater part of all oceans becomes a possible launching zone against any country; and it is impossible, for the moment, to envisage any effective search system, even the most futuristic, that could cover such a wide area.

On the other hand, the times of sailing and returning to harbour could conceivably present some opportunity for offensive ASW operations, given ASW means somewhat superior to those of today. But one very important reservation should be made: during such potentially vulnerable periods, an SSBN is not yet (or no longer) a playable piece on the chess-board of deterrence: only SSBNs actually on patrol can ensure deterrence. The question relates, therefore, to relatively marginal methods that would in the main be adopted at times of crisis and undeclared war. One solution, for a nation concerned with the safety of its SSBNs sailing for patrol and returning to harbour, would be to reinforce the protection it already affords to their movements and perhaps to establish below the air—sea interface, in the necessary areas, an ASW complex of the type discussed earlier. But, if an enemy broke this complex, there would be a fight; and a battle for or against the freedom of action of SSBNs is one of the possibilities of naval warfare that can be foreseen. Once again, it is hard to see how such a battle could lead to a first, pre-emptive, anti-force strike that could disarm at one blow all the enemy's means of launching a retaliatory strategic strike. None the less, the possibility is worth thinking about.

Formerly, the attack and defence of seaborne commerce involved only merchant ships or fishing vessels; maritime history is full of accounts of such fighting. But the growing importance and consequent vulnerability of maritime trade have already been pointed out. The attack-type submarine would seem to be a particularly formidable threat, especially if it is nuclear-propelled: its mobility, combined with the methods of satellite reconnaissance available to a number of navies today, makes the evasive tactics employed against the slow submarines of former times virtually useless. In the attack phase, this same mobility allows a nuclear submarine to close its target from any quarter and not only from the ahead sectors. This considerably increases the need for escorts. Moreover, the range of new submarine weapons permits attacks from long range — whence the necessity of greatly extending the depth of protective coverage. From these considerations, it is clear that the protection of maritime trade from SSNs requires enormous effort. The task is all the more formidable in the light of the proliferation of diesel-electric submarines throughout the world. These problems will be looked at again in part IV when the conduct of operations is discussed.

The attack and defence of forces at sea has already been dealt with in relation to SSBNs, and this also covers operations that take place in the approaches to ports and harbours. On the other hand, it is clearly difficult to separate underwater warfare from warfare above the surface simply for the convenience of argument. We shall therefore examine here just the problems of attacking and defending naval forces on the high seas or operating 'out of area'.

Submarine attacks against a naval force on the open seas share many of the features of attacks on merchant shipping. The difference is mainly one of degree: normally a naval force is faster, more manoeuvrable and better equipped for acoustic warfare, self-defence and counter-attack than a convoy of merchant vessels. In particular, warships may eventually be equipped with effective means of engaging sub-surface missiles during their air flight. And, although at the present time an SSN is superior in combat to the average surface vessel, this superiority is considerably diminished and can even be reversed if the naval force it attacks is formed so as to constitute a coherent, high-performance ASW system. None the less, in most cases the SSN makes it possible for the weak to attack the strong; and, correspondingly, a naval force, however powerful, will always have to reckon with the submarine threat. With the proliferation of submarines everywhere, this becomes true even for operations that only concern secondary nations. An amphibious operation, for example, is becoming less and less viable without anti-submarine protection.

To sum up the development of the role of the submarine, first of all the much greater possibilities for submarines now have opened up new fields of naval strategy and have altered some of the classical problems. Because they are now able to strike massively and directly at the heart of enemy territory, including a second strike, by means of the strategic missiles carried by SSBNs, submarine forces are bound to play an immediate and determinant role in the global strategic balance of power. The size of the threat that a nuclear submarine poses to merchant ships raises, in dramatic terms, the old problem of protecting merchant shipping in time of war for any nation dependent on it. The nuclear submarine has become a major actor in warfare between naval forces, which is affected in almost all its aspects by the development of submarines and anti-submarine warfare. Submarine development is one of the areas where competition between maritime nations is likely to become most keen.

In other respects, if fixed ground arrays prove effective, a notable new factor in naval strategy may emerge: naval warfare may become affected by questions of geography. In other words, the wide freedom of action hitherto enjoyed by fleets for surveillance and other naval operations almost anywhere in the oceans of the world may in future be restricted because, militarily speaking, the sea will no longer be uniform. This development could be very significant indeed.

The second traditional actor in naval warfare, the aircraft-carrier, must now be considered. The aircraft-carrier was the great victor in the Pacific war and in world opinion is probably the ultimate symbol of naval might. Whether a navy includes aircraft-carriers in its fleet or not is, rightly or wrongly, certainly a factor in deciding its rank. Aircraft-carriers are, none the less, the subject of keen controversy.

To begin with a comment of a general nature: even if this weapons system is usually described by the ship in which it is installed, an aircraft-carrier is nothing without the aircraft it operates. In practice, it would seem that this fact is not always clearly recognized. Technical developments among the many machines of war that are on the increase are nowhere so evident, so sophisticated or so costly as in fighter aircraft. This is even more true of carrier-borne combat aircraft for two simple reasons: the special conditions for operating them on board a ship impose severe limitations on their design; and, since fewer are required than land-based machines, carrier-borne aircraft of any given type are usually built in small numbers, with the consequent commercial penalties. This makes things extremely difficult for most nations. The point is obvious when one measures, for example, the distance separating the American F 14, which is capable of engaging several enemies at once out to a range of 100 nautical miles, from all its rivals.

We now turn to examine the capabilities of an aircraft-carrier used against land territories, commercial assets at sea and naval forces — which here too are clearly the pre-eminent stakes of warfare. An attack (as opposed to an ASW) aircraft-carrier retains a remarkable aptitude for carrying out destructive raids on shore, particularly if it carries nuclear weapons. It can also serve as a means of lifting troops ashore during an amphibious operation if it has helicopters suitable for this purpose, and it can be very valuable in ensuring subsequent logistic support of various kinds including medical services.

Against merchant vessels or naval forces it likewise has excellent offensive possibilities: if it has the requisite aircraft it can, above all, perform the essential reconnaissance function against surface vessels and mount an early-warning guard against aircraft. It can also provide, in a more limited fashion, a lookout for submarines with fixed-wing aircraft or helicopters. It can attack any surface target and support its raiding aircraft with electronic warfare. Finally it can intercept enemy aircraft at long range at all levels of violence because, in a situation of limited violence, it can positively identify the enemy and manoeuvre so as to prevent the enemy from closing and identifying its own forces. The capacity of carrier aircraft for aerial combat enables a carrier to spread a wide protective net against an air threat. In short, the aircraft-carrier is an admirable multi-purpose combatant. At the same time it is a ship that is particularly well suited to making a show of force in times of crisis.

But, of course, these are maximum capabilities not possessed by all aircraft-carriers. In light of such notable advantages, what are an aircraft-carrier's problems? The first is undoubtedly the sheer size brought about by technological developments. If it is to remain queen of the sea, it needs very good aircraft for ASW and surface reconnaissance, for keeping an air guard, for amphibious support, for air combat and for electronic warfare. Such aircraft weigh 20 tonnes, 27 tonnes, 30 tonnes, even 38 tonnes. Weights like these and the need to operate aircraft in all weather conditions demand gigantic platforms. This is a handicap, firstly because of the necessary burden on the supporting infrastructure and secondly because of the military and political disadvantages of concentrating so many resources in a single target — primarily because of the resulting vulnerability. This vulnerability arises, or will arise one day, from the relative ease with which satellites can spy out these gigantic ships.

It is worth pausing for a moment to consider why, in fact, aircraft-carriers up until now have been so resistant to criticism on the grounds of vulnerability. This is mainly because they were difficult to find. The mechanism was as follows. Since the search vehicle *par excellence* is a reconnaissance or patrol aircraft that can transform itself into a vehicle for holding contact and marking offensive units, the first thing an aircraft-carrier has always done is to shoot down any reconnaissance aircraft as soon as possible and thus remain secure. Then, if attacking aircraft are, all the same, dispatched on the basis of some rather stale information given by a patrol aircraft before it was shot down, the attackers have a choice. Either they can close at high altitude to optimize relocation, but at the risk of being themselves attacked by fighters from the carrier before they get within attacking range; or, instead, they can come in as low as possible so as to be able to close more safely but at the cost of not gaining detection until the last minute before their attack. During the low-altitude flight, the carrier, which will usually have had some warning of the raid before the aircraft went low and may even still be tracking them with AEW aircraft, can take evasive action which could very well succeed in misleading the attackers.

However, if total coverage by satellites, referred to above, is one day available, this ploy will no longer work. A carrier's size will make it very difficult for it to escape almost continuous surveillance. At the very least, it will have to burden itself with various deception devices. If it is located, its size again makes it easy to attack. And if it is, by its nature, pretty well protected against air attack it is much less able to defend itself against missiles and submarines. In view of the number of missiles that can attack it simultaneously, a carrier must be exceptionally well defended, either by weighing itself down with more armaments if that is practicable, or by having a much stronger escort than in the old days. Faced with modern submarines, for which its size makes it the ideal target, a complex and expensive apparatus is necessary to ensure any degree of effective defence.

On the whole it appears, therefore, that to ensure the safety of an aircraft-carrier in the presence of an enemy equipped with modern offensive weapons, while still maintaining its offensive capabilities, requires an increasingly heavy and high-performance aero-naval ensemble such as few navies can afford. If these conditions can be achieved, the aircraft-carrier remains a remarkable embodiment of naval power. It goes without saying that it is still particularly valuable for certain kinds of limited war.

Let us now see what has become of the traditional surface ship. Although people are accustomed to think of this foot-soldier of the sea as constituting the bulk of a fleet, its present position in modern warfare must be considered carefully — in particular, its fighting capability. In the last war surface ships were, in fact, closely rivalled by aircraft; if they made an important contribution to the defeat of the U-boat, that was only in so far as they formed part of a co-ordinated and complex system where the aircraft played an equally important role.

However, what has never changed is the importance of the surface ship in the complicated game of gaining control of the sea, with all that that entails: providing a presence in peacetime, in the economic field, in international or in foreign waters; its ability to take part in all kinds of action during a crisis; and its political influence. Thus it retains the ability to fulfil the special role of warship, such as was described earlier. Neither has the surface ship ever lost its multi-purpose nature, mainly because, unlike the submarine and the aircraft, it is in the sea and in the air at one and the same time. This enables it to receive all kinds of data, to make the best possible assessment of any given situation and to participate in all types of action. Hence a surface ship is well suited to co-ordination and command.

But how well is it fitted for engaging shore targets, commerce at sea or naval forces? Here the surface ship is undergoing a process of change that is still far from being complete. Against shore targets, it retains the limited possibilities afforded by conventional gunfire, but with a lesser capability than before because fewer guns are generally carried. But a considerable revival of fire-power could come about with certain types of missile, and in particular cruise missiles with nuclear warheads where these are included in the armament. Against commercial shipping, it is clearly as effective as ever. However, naval ships can no longer rely on being faster than merchant ships, and they are not suited to defending fixed installations.

Against naval forces, although the surface ship is now less well placed in an encounter with an SSN, it is now better able to react quickly against an attacking submarine, provided it is integrated in an ASW system that deprives the submarine of its trump cards. In face of airborne attacks, whether from an aircraft or a missile launched from land, a ship or an aircraft, surface-to-air missiles have already made a properly equipped ship a very well-defended target; and the likelihood of future progress in this area should allow it to maintain its position against this threat when the various technical problems have been solved.

Against its opposite number on the surface, its future is dependent on the missile's future and its fighting ability depends on an anti-ship missile with some kind of sea-air system: it could then find itself able to fulfil its traditional role. However, it is worth considering the possibility of missiles eventually having heads that are themselves capable to some extent of searching for, relocating and identifying a target. A device of this kind would give a surface ship many of the current advantages of the ship-and-embarked-aircraft tandem — that is, the ability to see and strike at long range, particularly if the missile is employed in conjunction with a search system that can reveal the approximate position of the enemy. A surface ship carrying such missiles does not need to have the enormous dimensions of an aircraft-carrier; and both the risks and the political presence can be distributed among a number of small ships over a wider area, even though surface ships would none the less not have the multi-purpose quality of the aircraft-carrier. It may well be that this is the kind of formula the Soviet navy is counting on to oppose American carriers. Incidentally, the ship-borne helicopter, which will be discussed later, has also helped to make the surface ship more effective.

Thus missiles, data processing and helicopters have restored standard surface ships to their rightful place in combat at sea — something that would have seemed unlikely some years ago. All the same, they are more and more liable, albeit to a lesser degree than aircraft-carriers, to constant surveillance.

Mine warfare has been significant in this century's conflicts. The mine itself has steadily progressed, with more and more ingenious firing systems that are sensitive to magnetic fields and acoustic or sea-pressure effects as well as to physical contact. Mines also can now be used at great depths, and the threat they can exert has thus been greatly extended.

Consequently the traditional minesweeper, which simulates the effect of the actual target vessel in order to explode a mine prematurely, has found it difficult to keep up with these developments. Hence the minehunter: being neutralized and not concerned with the mode of detonation, this makes a direct search and then detonates the mine deliberately. Its success can be judged by the fact that each year minehunters discover numerous Second World War mines that minesweepers had passed over to no purpose. The minehunter is efficient today, but its effectiveness will lessen when the mine has in turn been made harder to detect. The future might see, perhaps, a combination of minehunter and minesweeper, or something evolved from the latter based on simulating target influences.

It is necessary, furthermore, to take note of an important new factor in mine warfare that has come about with the development of real possibilities for the use of mines in offensive operations. This is primarily the result of the increased effectiveness of the submarine, but it also relates to another new factor which, although not naval, could play an important role here — heavy cargo aircraft, with a large radius of action, which could lay a large number of mines in enemy waters in a short time.

Thus the mine will, for a long time yet, be an important

component of naval warfare, both when used offensively and as a means of defence. The ability to utilize mines or to set up defences against them is therefore still an important way of limiting an enemy's strategic freedom of action and of safeguarding one's own movements.

Finally we turn to naval aircraft. The development of carrier-borne aircraft has already been noted and needs no further discussion, but two very important types of naval aircraft have yet to be considered. The maritime-patrol aircraft is still one of the essential tools of military action at sea: indeed, it is the most usual instrument of search and reconnaissance, a task that has already been shown to be of the highest importance. A patrol aircraft has no difficulty in detecting surface ships but merely has to take care not to get shot down. On the other hand, it will be competing more and more with satellites, although it will always be better at making positive identification and, above all, at holding contact. Against nuclear submarines, its radar and passive electronic detection systems are almost impotent, but acoustic and magnetic detection devices remain effective. A necessary intermediary for acoustic detection is the sonobuoy, which can be passive or active, and which is being improved all the time. In magnetic-anomaly detection equipment (MAD), progress is more restricted but, as has been said above, MAD is capable of forcing a submarine to go deep in order to avoid being relocated. In addition, as with the surface ship, a patrol aircraft's fighting role has been enhanced by the missiles it can carry.

As for the naval helicopter, its attraction lies in its potential for achieving the ship-aircraft tandem with far less tonnage than the combination of carrier and fixed-wing aircraft. It is also well suited for surface search, trans-horizon missile guidance for surface-to-surface attacks by ships carrying the requisite weapons, detection of submarines by MAD and sonar, and anti-submarine attacks with torpedoes. In search and surface-attack missions, however, it is very far from being a rival to fixed-wing aircraft. At present, the more common fire-control radars have difficulty in acquiring a helicopter target when it is down close to the sea surface; but it will be a much easier target for future radars and its fragility makes it much more vulnerable than a normal aircraft. Although it is currently invaluable in anti-submarine warfare, it will be eventually limited by its load-carrying capacity. Thus among the other naval actors the helicopter is a worthy contributor to operations, but it is not a panacea.

In summary, the forces which could fight at sea today or in the near future appear to be distinguished by the following important developments:

1 The strategic deployment of naval forces, formerly secret, are probably about to be affected by the revolution in search and reconnaissance which could be brought about by satellite observation and passive-listening ground arrays, but about which not much is publicly known. Meanwhile, long deployments are made easier by the fact that ships have become a good deal more self-sufficient.
2 All the actors in naval warfare today would approach the scene of combat already engaged in a complex preliminary manoeuvre in which numerous methods of collecting intelligence are set against the methods for confusing or deceiving them in various ways. The technical and intellectual mastery of this phase of naval action is becoming essential to success in combat.
3 Fighting itself would be radically changed by the ubiquity of the threat of attack, which could come at any moment from near or far, from the sky or sea-surface or from underwater, above all in the shape of missiles of higher and higher performance and more and more varied capabilities — and, one day, doubtless in the shape of even more futuristic weapons.

8

THE CONSEQUENCES FOR NAVAL STRATEGY

The consequences of the changes outlined above for naval strategy can be grouped in three categories: those that affect the general features of naval warfare; those that modify the principles of naval action; and those that will lead to future changes.

With regard to the effect on general features of naval warfare, two aspects stand out: the role of geographical factors is altered; and there have been various changes in dimension which themselves generate secondary consequences. One change in the role of geographical factors is that the dependence of fleets on shore naval bases has altered. For a deployment lasting from several weeks to several months, dependence on overseas bases has decreased on account of the steady development of strategic mobility. Distant bases are no longer as necessary to the conduct of operations as they were. On the other hand, over longer periods dependence has if anything increased, because the scope for repairs on board is either inhibiting or makes it necessary to buy replacements abroad locally and expensively or else to rely on air transport. Correspondingly, the demand for well-stocked bases at home has increased. Another important consequence of a geographical nature is that the feasibility of action from shore to sea has greatly increased both in range and in effectiveness. This is due to:

1 The much greater potential of surface-to-surface missiles and of means of detection that allows them to engage a target further and further away from land

2 The increased capabilities of land-based aircraft
3 The possibility of carrying light surface-to-surface missiles on fast motor-boats, which would confer a formidable ability to defend any coast that offered hiding-places and shelter from the roughest seas
4 The further development of fixed ground-array sonar networks, first at points where ships have to pass, and then in those deep-water areas where the concern for detecting enemy vessels, especially submarines, is greatest
5 The growing economic interests in the sea and on the seabed, illustrated today by the expansion of 'exclusive trade areas' and by the tendency of states to appropriate whole sea areas.

Various factors of dimension have undergone spectacular developments. In the dimension of space, the increased range of both detection and weapons and the enlarged field of action of all the platforms have, in effect, shrunk the seas. In the dimension of time, vessels are faster, there is greater readiness for attack, and reaction times are shorter. Another change of dimension has taken place in the scale of material resources necessary for a major participant in naval warfare; they have been obvious throughout this review but, for convenience, a list of 'key resources' is appended to this section. Finally, there has been an increase in the minimum size of a naval force that can ensure its own protection against all kinds of threat while retaining its offensive capacity. Formerly, a single ship had this capability; today it can only be achieved by a complex assembly, such as will be described later.

These changes in dimension might have far-reaching consequences. The conduct of naval action has to adapt itself to such changes; we shall try to go more deeply into this further on. The gap between small and large naval powers has widened. It is no longer only a matter of having a greater or lesser number of those elements which were formerly the common denominator in any navy — ships. It is more a matter of having, or not having, such and such a type of key means. This, together with the change of dimension undergone by the minimum force capable of protecting itself while still acting offensively, has brought about a kind of threshold of naval power relating to the possession or non-possession of what might be called an elementary naval unit, whose definition is that it has a wide enough range of resources to be capable of both offence and defence; the composition of such a unit will be suggested in the next chapter. In consequence, fewer and fewer navies will have a complete range of strategic options at their disposal.

Such, then, are the probable changes affecting the general features of naval warfare. How may these developments affect the principles of naval action itself? Of note here are, on the one hand, the position of naval action among other types of action (whether military or not) in which a given government is involved, and, on the other, the effect on the traditional principles of operating naval forces.

In the present political-strategic scenario, and in view of the complexity of naval actors today, the position of naval operations as part of the whole game is not easy to define. The first part of this study described a state of low tension, with its accompanying activities — political presence and preparation for assuming control of the sea; crisis, with its confrontation of wills; and various kinds of actual warfare. Chapter 4 went on to review the various characteristics of naval operations, these being constituents of systems whose technical conclusion, sooner or later, is wholesale destruction of the enemy, hence fighting, hence acts of war. These systems have their own logic, which is based on technical and quantifiable considerations. But is this logic absolutely consistent with the logic of actual situations?

In open war between two sides that are face to face, the answer can be 'yes', if due allowance is made for the variety of possible combat situations. At the other extreme — that is, in a period of low tension — the reply may equally be 'yes' because, so far as the logic of naval operational systems is concerned, tension is, above all, a state of constant readiness; and that is common to both situations — war and tension. And the requirements which those situations may engender are, as a rule, fairly easy to satisfy. The most difficult situation lies between the two extremes — in crisis and at the borderline between crisis and war.

Firstly, with regard to a serious nuclear crisis, thinking

generally steers, like a ship in a buoyed channel, between two lines of danger. The first danger is that of minimizing the true role of crisis in nuclear-age confrontations and proceeding too quickly to war by treating deterrence lightly. The second is to take the opposite view and favour deterrence to the extent of invalidating all thoughts on the subject of war and concluding that actual fighting is purely hypothetical, and further and further removed from reality.

Crises can arise from various causes which need not be stated again. But, militarily speaking, crisis has an exact meaning: it is, in fact, a limited trial of strength, whether or not blood is shed, intended to ensure the ultimate effectiveness of deterrence. This implies means and behaviour which pose a particular military problem. It would seem, however, that a crisis can succeed — that is, achieve its essential goal of preserving deterrence — only if a contingent path to war is made ready, studied in depth and even accepted to some degree. Indeed, one cannot dismiss the possibility that a power might envisage total war. And if that power felt it was greatly superior in its capacity to wage war, even nuclear war, against an enemy who trusted too much in the deterrent and therefore had somewhat neglected to prepare for war, it could speculate on the chances of taking such an enemy by storm and overwhelming him so quickly that he would not be able to retaliate. To prevent the exposure of such a weakness, it is vital to persuade a potential enemy that he will meet with effective opposition at all stages and all points; and the processes of governmental decision making must be seen to be coherent and convincing in this respect. Thus a direct capacity for deterrence based on strategic nuclear missiles and the contingent ability to fight a modern nuclear war, which would have to be conducted in an evolving and complex technological environment, would both seem to be necessary if naval operations are to receive their full significance in a situation of serious crisis where fate is finely balanced between war and a rational return to non-war.

As regards the less serious naval crisis, which has earlier been termed continual because, especially during the past 35 years, numerous instances have occurred (and still occur), this also presents a serious difficulty: it is necessary not only to appreciate a political-strategic situation correctly, in order to discern the margin of manoeuvre available before falling into risk of war, but also to select modes of action that are most appropriate for obtaining the desired political result. This type of crisis has, moreover, its own technical and tactical requirements, which are different from those demanded by total war. The key points are reliable intelligence, excellent communications, a convincing appearance and the ability to remain at sea. (This will be returned to in the final chapter, in connection with the decisions that have to be made in advance of a naval operation.) All in all, this type of crisis is of major importance in the world today.

After thus placing naval action within a strategic whole, we can now consider what effect the developments reviewed have on the three classical preoccupations (which amount to principles of war) of strategists faced with the problem of operating their forces — maintaining freedom of action, achieving economy of effort and using concentration of force to make the best of any favourable imbalance.

Freedom of action depends on a number of basic requirements:

1 *Mobility.* As we have seen, forces are becoming more mobile; in particular, nuclear propulsion has spectacularly increased submarines' mobility.
2 *The ability to make strategic moves secretly.* This is rapidly decreasing world-wide, as methods of search improve.
3 *Real freedom of the sea.* This has been reduced on account of states' tendency to appropriate sea areas to themselves and because of modern weapon technology which makes such appropriation a reality by affording effective methods of policing the seas and fighting if need be, especially in confined waters.
4 *The state of nuclear deterrence.* Basically, deterrence limits freedom of action for those who practise it because it prevents them from embarking on certain ventures; on the other hand, it gives a nation that practises deterrence a certain marginal freedom of action in relation to secondary nations with no nuclear deterrent to the extent that deterrence guards against the principal threat. Of course, other countries can profit from the limitations that deterrence imposes on the freedom of action of two nuclear nations opposed to each other. In the

free space left by these limitations there is often room for action by a third power; this is significant in situations of continual crisis discussed earlier.

5 *Real 'control of the sea'.* In general, increased mobility has brought about an increase in the interpenetration of fleets in peacetime; and control of the sea is therefore sometimes a little precarious. In any case, so-called 'control of the sea' has lost a good deal of its meaning, since strategic missiles can make a mockery of any enemy devices placed between them and their target.

So it appears that powers that avail themselves of 'key resources' have greater freedom of action because they alone are able to see the whole picture and because, by reason of quantitative and, more important, qualitative superiority, they are able to send their forces everywhere where their chief enemy does not actively oppose them. On the other hand, the rest have less freedom of action wherever war is rife between the great powers; but there are still some good opportunities for action by enterprising navies at times of continual crisis or cold war.

The capacity for concentration, as a principle of war, has been immensely improved, partly as a result of increased mobility. In this respect it must be emphasized that nuclear attack-class submarines (SSNs) can now operate as a co-ordinated team. A more important factor in the increased ability to achieve concentration, however, is the advent of long-range missiles: it is enough to bring these to bear on the assigned targets to achieve a formidable concentration of fire. This is obviously true of strategic systems and is likely to be equally true of tactical systems in the future.

Economy of effort is obviously changing in relation to the means which are evolving in naval warfare; however, it would seem that the problem in principle is unchanged, since no power, however great, has sufficient means to do everything, everywhere at the same time. Economy of effort is therefore more important than ever.

The effect of the various developments on the main principles involved in operating a force appears, therefore, to be a movement towards a diversification in freedom of action to the profit of the largest navies and the detriment of the smallest, at least in wartime; towards increased possibilities for concentration; and towards maintaining economy of effort as a principle of war.

What are the long-term prospects arising from recent technical developments? The abundance and variety of technological advances promise such a proliferation of future innovations that they could not possibly be listed. Two possibilities, however, merit particular attention. On the one hand, the importance of satellites — for communications, navigation and reconnaissance — has grown so much that it is hard to believe there will not be, in addition to land, air and water, a fourth element where war may be waged in the future: outer space. On the other hand, developments in data processing, long-range weapons and methods of search and detection suggest that military systems could increasingly develop independently of the platforms of those systems. Already, for example, a missile directed at a ship target is tending to become one and the same weapon, whether launched from the surface, the sky or from the depths of the sea. Missiles could, perhaps, soon be launched from land, even if the target is far out to sea, if the missiles themselves are able to locate and identify.

It is clear that the influence of these various developments on the actors in a naval operation takes many forms. Various kinds of confrontation could evolve, such as were envisaged in the first chapter, on the reasonably uniform foundation constituted by the marine environment and the basic characteristics of the warship. These confrontations would involve actors that have themselves undergone radical change: territories tending towards urban and sometimes industrial concentrations; commercial assets at sea vastly increasing in quantity and importance, and growing in diversity; and naval forces that are themselves constantly diversifying and improving.

The range of what is now possible has also opened wide. At the least intense level of confrontation — a state of low tension, continuing crisis or cold war — naval action is dominated by political appraisals of the situation. Very often this involves actors that are not all visible: the superpowers, rarely indifferent to tension and crisis, play their part through the intermediary of their subsidies, advisers and weapons, if not their armed forces, and yet they are restrained by mutual opposition. Their role is thus significant, but it is not exclusive and is, moreover, difficult to evaluate. Ideologies, national feelings, economic constraints and a good many other factors are added to military constraints to make this kind of situation a difficult but fertile ground for naval operations that are strictly tied to the pursuit of political designs. Technically, naval action in such circumstances poses special problems, but it benefits from technical progress in operational intelligence, communications and endurance at sea. On the other hand, a naval actor in such a situation is less susceptible to the need for sophisticated weapon systems. It is therefore evident that at this level of confrontation — which, at the time of writing, is the most important, since it actually exists — many navies have the capacity to play a part because the possession of the most sophisticated and most costly systems is not indispensable.

A serious nuclear crisis, on the other hand, is a much tougher kind of confrontation because mistakes here could be much more costly; because it poses vast technological and tactical problems which are much more difficult to solve; and because, by definition, it involves opposing powers with considerable means at their disposal. To the extent that a high degree of war readiness, of which the enemy must be made aware, is necessary here for a belligerent who wants to deter as well as for one who wants to attack, a crisis of this kind involves problems, systems and equipment not far removed from those dictated by total war. Although, of course, this kind of crisis mostly concerns nuclear powers, their allies or their clients, indeed even neutral neighbours in confrontation areas, can also be involved. Furthermore, we cannot forget that nuclear proliferation could eventually multiply the number of occasions when a nuclear crisis could rear its head, perhaps along very different lines from those to which everyone has become accustomed during the past 30 years or more of East—West cold war.

In certain cases of limited war without nuclear weapons, SSNs or reconnaissance satellites, operations could take on a collective appearance not dissimilar to that of the last war despite technological advances: a war like this could be fought between non-nuclear powers, or with a single nuclear power behaving like a non-nuclear power, provided the objectives did not formally affect the ultimate balance between the superpowers.

Other cases of limited war, involving major powers in naval warfare along the lines envisaged in part I, could resemble the last war in some ways, notably during combat; but they would be very different in other respects because the antagonists would have purpose-built equipment for surveillance and reconnaissance, they would have SSNs, and they would also have the whole range of missiles and electronic warfare equipment. This kind of war, albeit limited by reason of nuclear weapons not being used, would be much more technical, much shorter and probably more deadly than the last war, wherever it took place. On the other hand — a notable difference — it would probably spare the 'sanctuaries', and, of course, the nuclear sword of Damocles would constantly hang over it because nothing would guarantee that its limited nature would last to the end. It would therefore probably be a highly political affair, and operations would have to stick close to diplomatic moves.

Before going on, in this review of possible confrontations, to a higher level of violence, it must be emphasized that such a war would imply failure, perhaps not irremediable but certainly very serious, for the countries that want deterrence and believe in its effectiveness. This carries the important practical implication that, logically, the countries concerned would have done everything beforehand to avoid the threshold being crossed.

The successive stages of naval warfare would look entirely different from those that so far have been envisaged. Firstly, they would be dominated by SSBN operations for which nuclear countries would, at any price, have to keep freedom of action. The run-up to actual fighting with respect to those operations would be a game of evasion, in the course of which each side would be obsessed with the possibility both of finding itself suddenly under fire from the enemy and of obtaining permission from its own government to open fire. So far as combat is concerned, probably nuclear by now, it would be like nothing ever seen before. Nevertheless, it is unlikely that there would be only a frenzied and disordered outbreak of fighting. The preparedness, judgement and composure of the people involved and the quality of the equipment and tactics would play a decisive part; and purpose-built systems, the appearance of which has already been noted, would now realize their full potential. What might follow such fighting leaves the field of technical developments and their consequences, which this part of the book has covered, and brings us back to the alternatives suggested in part I — restoration of the deterrent or continuation of the fighting.

Finally it should be emphasized that, although this summary of the situations that can be envisaged, with all their technical implications, has treated them separately for the purposes of the argument, in reality they may overlap one another, interact with one another, and so on.

APPENDIX TO PART III

THE PRINCIPAL KEY RESOURCES IN NAVAL OPERATIONS

Search

Naval surveillance and reconnaissance satellites
Passive sonar ground arrays
Multi-purpose maritime-patrol aircraft
Anti-surface maritime-patrol aircraft
Modern DF arrays
Helicopters equipped for search

Ship-borne sensors

Modern radar
Modern active sonar
Modern passive sonar
EW intercept equipment covering all frequencies

Weapons

Long-range surface-to-surface missiles able to relocate and identify
Surface-to-surface missiles without an identification capacity
Surface-to-air missiles for engaging all aircraft in service
High-performance anti-missile systems
Improved conventional weapons
Laser and neutron weapons
Missiles undergoing two changes of medium (e.g. sub-surface to surface to sub-surface)
Missiles undergoing one change of medium (e.g. sub-surface to surface)
Active electronic warfare equipment

Command and control

Communication-satellite systems
Navigation-satellite systems
High-performance data processing

Units

The possession of one or more 'elementary naval unit'
Submarines
- SSBNs
- General-purpose SSNs
- Anti-surface SSNs
- Diesel-electric SSKs

Aircraft-carriers
- General purpose
- Restricted capability

High-performance surface ships
Mine warfare
- Minehunters
- Minesweepers
- Offensive long-range minelaying aircraft

Fast missile-attack craft
Amphibious-landing ships
Seagoing logistic-support ships
- All areas
- Restricted areas

HMS *Hermes*, flagship of Rear Admiral J. F. Woodward, commander of the Falkland Islands Task Force during the British—Argentinian confrontation in 1982 — a limited war which demonstrated clearly that naval warfare is indeed possible today and, perhaps, tomorrow. (Note the weapons park on the deck forward.) (Ministry of Defence)

The Harrier deck park on *Hermes* in snowy weather, May 1982, at morning flying stations. (Note the RAF GR3s aft.) (Ministry of Defence)

3 Aegis guided missile cruiser USS *Ticonderoga* during her first sea trials in May 1982. With four powerful gas-turbines driving two shafts to give a speed of more than 30 knots this class of guided missile cruiser is exceptionally well equipped in all respects for missile and electronic warfare in practically any environment. However, the class is not as self-sufficient as its nuclear-propelled equivalents. (US Navy)

4 Attack aircraft carrier USS *Independence* surrounded by other ships of the Mediterranean task force in December 1970. The escort shown here is by no means indicative of what is required in war to guard against the threat from the surface, from below the surface and from the air, with missiles coming from all sources. (US Navy)

The battleship USS *New Jersey* just before recommissioning in January 1983. Though scarcely a high-performance surface ship — one of the 'key resources' — her heavy armament would nevertheless be useful in certain kinds of limited war, especially for shore bombardment, but above all as an excellent command and communications platform. (US Navy)

A battle fleet of the past: the US fleet lying at anchor in Guantanamo Bay, Cuba *c.*1927. (US Navy)

7 The nuclear-powered general purpose aircraft carrier USS *Dwight D. Eisenhower* in the Gulf of Mexico just before a major fleet exercise in January 1979. Requiring no refuelling and capable of self-maintenance, a carrier like this can remain at sea for extended periods but her own defensive missile armament is not sufficient to protect her from all threats and a substantial escort would be needed in war. The cost of such a ship (over $2000 million) puts it out of reach of any but the superpowers. (US Navy)

8 NATO ships anchored at Spithead in June 1969. The wide variety of 'foot soldiers of the sea' is readily apparent. (US Navy)

HMS *Brecon,* one of the mine countermeasures vessels whose value is likely to increase as mine warfare assumes greater significance in the future. (Ministry of Defence)

The Soviet helicopter cruiser *Moskva* in the Mediterranean in February 1980 with HMS *Intrepid* in the background. With a primary anti-submarine role, and clearly an eye on SSNs and SSBNs, the two ships of this class have an anti-air warning and missile defence system; but, perhaps most importantly (especially in the Soviet Navy), *Moskva* is very well equipped for command and control. (Ministry of Defence)

11 Part of the Falklands Task Force in April 1982 being led by a nuclear submarine on the surface — by no means an SSN's usual role! However, SSNs submerged, well ahead of a force, are a valuable means of defence against attacking submarines of all kinds, as well, indeed, as against a surface threat. (Ministry of Defence)

12 The US Sixth Fleet in the Mediterranean in formation during March 1976. The ships would have to be a great deal further apart, of course, if a nuclear threat developed. (US Navy)

3 A modern 'foot soldier of the sea': HMS *Broadsword,* a multi-purpose Type 22 frigate armed with four Exocet surface-to-surface missiles and two six-barrelled Sea Wolf surface-to-air missile launchers for self-defence against aircraft and anti-ship missiles. Six torpedo tubes fire Mk 46 anti-submarine torpedoes and two Lynx helicopters can carry either anti-ship missiles or anti-submarine torpedoes. (Ministry of Defence)

14, The nuclear-powered Soviet *Kiev,* a truly formidable general purpose aircraft
15 carrier with the addition of four twin SS-N-12 surface-to-surface missiles with a 550 km range capability; 16 reloads are carried. Guns and surface-to-air missiles comprise the point defence systems and *Kiev* has a powerful anti-submarine capability. The three ships of this class, outstandingly well fitted for command, control and communications, are ideally suited for intervention in times of so-called peace. (Ministry of Defence)

'Foot soldiers' of the Soviet Navy refuelling at sea: as the Soviet fleet increases its presence in distant waters so the need for logistical support is correspondingly increased. (Ministry of Defence)

Soviet Krivak II class frigate *Razitelnyi* at anchor off Solum, Libya in October 1979. Such units contribute a powerful political presence; it is significant that this photograph was taken by a Wessex 5 helicopter from HMS *Intrepid* which was also in the area. (Ministry of Defence)

18 The LPD *Ivan Rogov* (photographed in April 1980) is twice the displacement, at 12,500 tons, of previous Soviet amphibious landing ships and has a docking well for assault craft. There is accommodation for a battalion of naval infantry (522 men) and a maximum of 40 tanks can be carried. A twin-launcher for SA-N-4 missiles provides surface-to-air missile defence. (Ministry of Defence)

Soviet *Kashin* class destroyer *Smyshleny,* one of the attendant and necessary escorts for the carrier *Kiev* when the latter was operating off the north coast of Egypt in 1979. (Ministry of Defence)

Amphibious assault ship USS *Saipan* in September 1980 — another of the 'key resources' for naval operations. Extensive medical facilities are included in this class of LHA — an important point for prolonged operations. The floodable docking well beneath the after elevator accommodates four LCU 1610 landing craft; there is a large garage for vehicles and sufficient troop accommodation for a reinforced battalion. (US Navy)

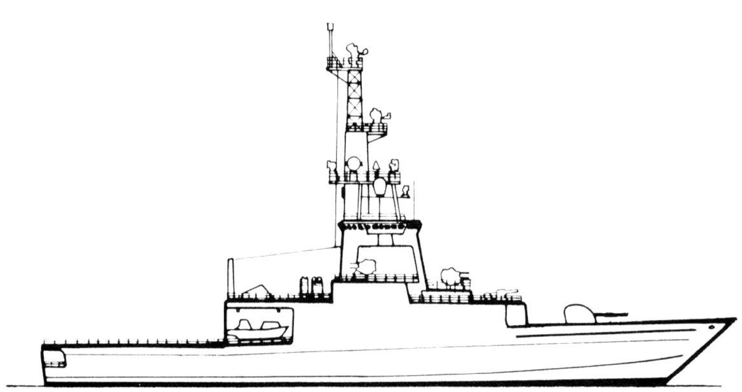

21, 1/43 'block' model and profile drawing of the S90. This controversial frigate-
22 design has been researched in answer to the requirements of the UK 1981 Defence White Paper. The ship is compact (length about 91.5 m) and broad (17.2 m on the water line) with a full load displacement of 2,800 tonnes. It is designed to carry a substantial weapon load including a heavy anti-aircraft gun, missile-armaments and torpedoes, plus up to two helicopters. It would be able to operate with stability in rough weather and to maintain speed of advance sufficient to protect a convoy (cruising endurance: 8,000 nautical miles at 16 knots; endurance at maximum power: 2,000 nautical miles at 28 knots). Relatively inexpensive to build, the S90 would be the most heavily armed ship (excluding aircraft carriers) in the Royal Navy. (Thornycroft-Giles & Associates)

HMS *Fearless* at Ascension Island in April 1982 on the way to the Falkland Islands. An RFA tug is alongside. *Fearless* and *Intrepid*, the Royal Navy's only amphibious assault ships, played a vital part in the Falklands conflict. Both were due to be sold under the Conservatives' defence review put forward by John Nott. (It was rumoured at the time that the Argentinians had expressed interest in buying HMS *Fearless*.) (Robert Fox)

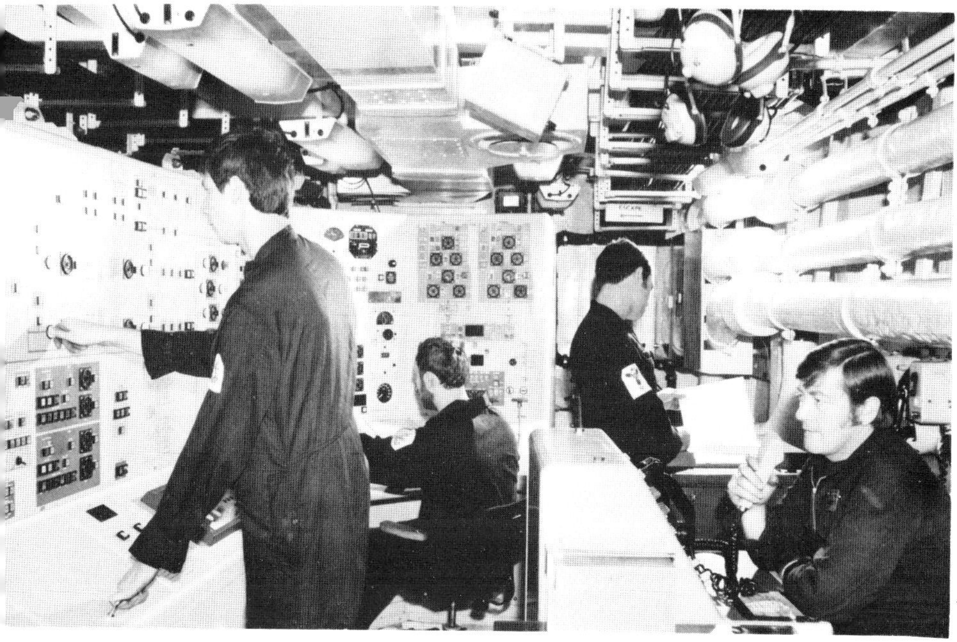

The Ship Control Centre in HMS *Broadsword* (Type 22). All main and auxiliary machinery is controlled from here and the economy in terms of manpower is obvious. (Ministry of Defence)

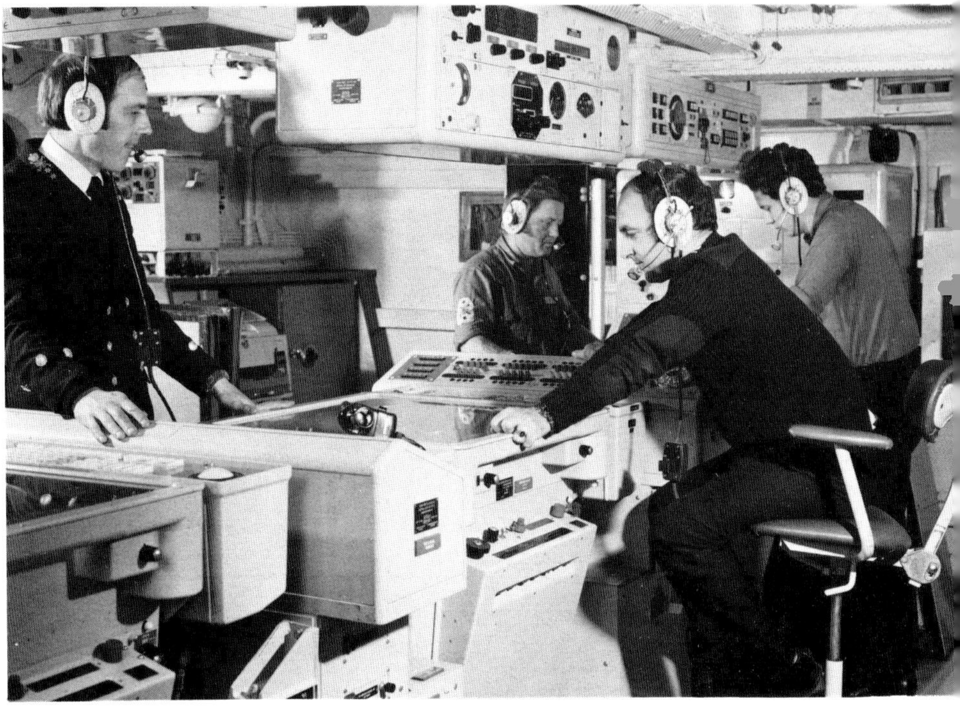

25 A section of the computer-assisted action information system in HMS *Cleopatra*'s operations room. An adequate computer is essential for rapid and accurate control of guns, missiles and anti-submarine weapons: the response of weapon systems to a threat, particularly from missiles, must be immediate. (Ferranti Computer Systems)

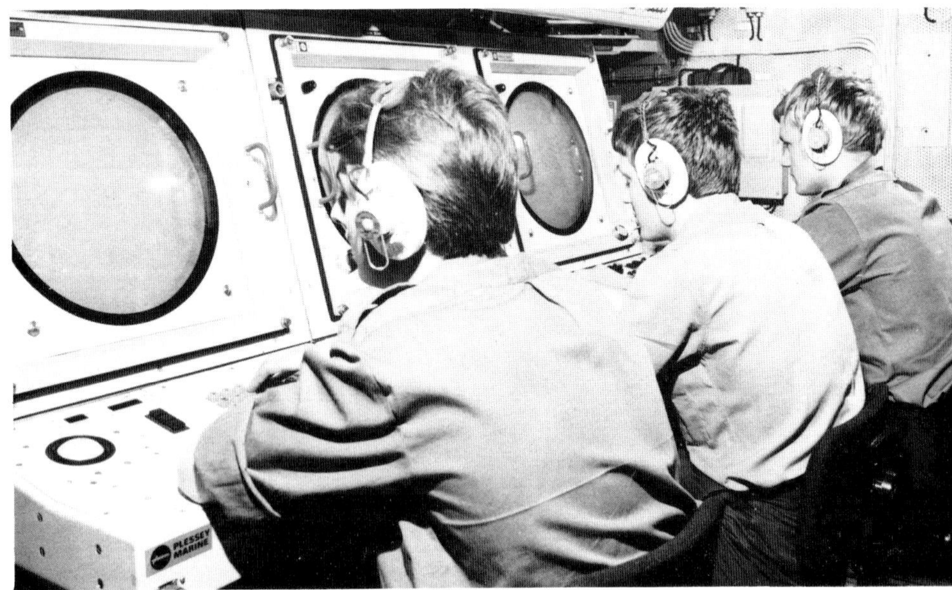

26 The display console of the Plessey Marine Type 2016 Fleet Escort Sonar on board HMS *Battleaxe*. (Plessey Marine)

The fleet replenishment ship *Resource* operating with the Falklands Task Force in 1982. Logistic support ships are, of course, essential for distant operations and vessels like *Resource* are well equipped for the rapid transfer of loads at sea, with modern handling methods and up to four Sea King helicopters. (Royal Navy Submarine Museum)

It is possible to fit certain merchant ships for troop transport and other military duties very quickly, as demonstrated at the outset of the Falklands conflict. It is only necessary to ratify and to put into effect agreements reached with shipping companies long before the state of tension requires any action to be taken. The liner *Queen Elizabeth* is shown here in the South Atlantic with the helicopter platform that was installed in only a few days using plans and drawings already available. (Royal Navy Submarine Museum)

29 Sea Harriers on the flight deck of HMS *Hermes* in the South Atlantic, 1982. These V/STOL strike fighters performed exceedingly well against Argentinian aircraft and shore targets; their success was evidence of the importance and effectiveness of an aircraft carrier (with adequate aircraft) in naval warfare today. Neither HMS *Hermes* nor HMS *Invincible* was equipped with a catapult; only helicopters and jump-jet Harriers (using the 'ski-jump' for take-off) could operate from the two ships. (Ministry of Defence)

30 Mirage 2000 armed with an ASMP air-to-surface missile giving a stand-off range capability of about 100 km. The ASMP carries a nuclear warhead with an estimated yield of 100 to 150 kilotons: thus this weapon system poses a formidable threat to surface forces if 'nuclear virginity' is broken. (Aerospatiale)

Super Etendard aircraft, particularly when armed with Exocet AM39 air-to-surface missiles, created a considerable problem of defence for the British Task Force Commander during the Falklands fighting and were responsible, *inter alia*, for sinking the first British ship to be lost, HMS *Sheffield*. (Aerospatiale)

US F-18A Hornet armed with Sidewinder (Wingtip) and Sparrow air-to-air missiles. Sidewinder with its infra-red homing system proved very effective when fired from British Harriers against Argentinian aircraft in 1982. (US Navy)

33 US Tomcat designed primarily as a carrier-based aircraft for protecting a strike force in contested airspace with support from early-warning aircraft and surface ships. It also has a ground-attack role and can carry a combination of missiles and bombs. Equipped with ECM, including chaff dispensers and integral jammers, it is well advanced in the field of electronic warfare. (US Navy)

34 A standard day in the South Atlantic 1982, seen from HMS *Hermes* with HMS *Broadsword* — a defensive 'goalkeeper' against air and missile attack — in the background. Aircraft and weapon systems stood up remarkably well to the foul weather. (Ministry of Defence)

The flight deck of HMS *Hermes* on a cold, frosty South Atlantic morning in 1982 with a Harrier ready in the launch position. (Ministry of Defence)

Sea Harrier landing on board HMS *Invincible* after a Combat Air Patrol (CAP) mission. During the Falklands campaign 28 Sea Harriers flew 2380 sorties and were in the air for 2680 hours: they destroyed at least 27 Argentinian aircraft in air-to-air combat without suffering any casualties, but two Harriers were brought down by fire from the ground and three were lost in accidents. (Ministry of Defence)

37 One of the 'key resources' for surveillance — a long-range Maritime Patrol Nimrod keeps an eye on the Soviet aircraft carrier *Kiev* off the West coast of Scotland in 1980. (Ministry of Defence)

38 Nimrod Mk III Airborne Early Warning (AEW). All-round coverage is ensured by radar scanners mounted at either end of the airframe. The pulsed Doppler radar has a good ship surveillance capability besides detecting aircraft out to long ranges. Sophisticated anti-jamming features are incorporated in the system and data control is computerized and, for the most part, fully automatic. (Ministry of Defence)

One of the increasing number of commercial assets at sea besides merchant vessels — an oil exploratory rig off Wick with an Anti-Submarine Warfare (ASW) Nimrod Mk II flying past. (Ministry of Defence)

40 British O-class patrol submarines have an excellent diesel-electric system that, although not giving them a speed and endurance comparable with nuclear power, is extremely quiet on main motors submerged. It is also sufficiently quiet when snorting (snorkelling) to guard against passive detection for a long while yet, if commanding officers adopt correct tactics. (Royal Navy Submarine Museum)

One of the first large post-war diesel-electric submarines built by the USSR, a *Zulu IV,* seen here on patrol in April 1979. Much more heavily dependent on the atmosphere than modern patrol-class submarines, it cannot be expected that a boat of this kind would be effective or survive for long. (Ministry of Defence)

French *Agosta* diesel-electric submarine. Submerged, boats of this type are quiet although they have a very limited performance at the top speed of 20 knots. Patrol submarines have by no means yet been perfected and further improvements can be expected. Their present slow speed of advance, especially if wanting to remain undetected, means very early deployment in times of tension. (ECP Armées)

43 French *Daphne* class patrol submarine approaching the ice edge. These boats are well armed with twelve 550 mm (21.7 in) torpedo tubes and they have an operational diving depth of 300 m (984 ft) with a crushing depth of 575 m (1886 ft). Now 15—20 years old, they are little better than Second World War German Type XXI U-Boats (which, in fact, never saw active service in war) and their capability in modern naval warfare where major navies are involved must be questioned. (ECP Armées)

44 French SSBN (SNLE) *Le Redoutable* diving. This is one of the five strategic ballistic-missile submarines which currently provide the French independent nuclear deterrent: two more will be operational in 1984 and 1990. The French Ministry of Defence aims to keep two SSBNs continuously on patrol and this requires six hulls. The 16 tubes amidships carry MSBS M-20 1500 n.m. (2743 km) missiles with megaton nuclear heads. Recognizing that this medium range restricts the areas of operation (with all that is implied by that), the French SSBNs will in due course be equipped with 4000 n.m. (7314 km) M4 missiles with 150 kiloton MIRV warheads. (ECP Armées)

5 French SSBN (SNLE) *Foudroyant*. Like the rest of her class this submarine is broadly similar to the British *Resolution* class, displacing 8940 tons dived and capable of about 25 knots submerged. The four 21 inch (532 mm) torpedo tubes are primarily intended for self-defence: it is no part of SSBN policy deliberately to seek tactical engagements. (ECP Armées)

USS *Houston* (SSN 713) in the Atlantic in August 1982. This is one of the *Los Angeles* class general purpose attack-type nuclear submarines with particular capability of coordinated operations with the surface ships and other units. Reputedly capable of diving to 450 m (1475 ft), these submarines have a top speed in excess of 30 knots and are heavily armed with SUBROC anti-submarine missiles and Mk 48 torpedoes. It is planned to fit this class with Tomahawk cruise missiles. (US Navy)

47 British SSBN of the *Resolution* class. Four submarines of this class were built to enable one to be constantly on patrol at sea — a patrol cycle that has been maintained since 1967. The increasing cost of refitting and updating these submarines is reflected by the £78 million spent on HMS *Renown*'s refit as against the £39.95 million it cost to build in 1964–68. It is because of this, as well as the desirability of carrying Trident missiles, that the new British Trident SSBN building programme is planned. (Royal Navy Submarine Museum)

48 Soviet *Juliett* class diesel-electric cruise-missile submarine armed with six 21 inch torpedo tubes and four surface-to-surface SS-N-3A missiles. The submarine must surface to launch the latter but their range is probably in excess of 450 km. (Ministry of Defence)

USS *Ohio* (SSBN 726) in the Atlantic, September 1981. This class of strategic missile submarine carries 24 Trident missiles which, in the Trident III version, will have a range of 9600 km (6000 miles). MARV (manoeuvring re-entry vehicle) nuclear warheads are being designed to evade ABM interception missiles to ensure still further that the deterrent force has the ability to strike at the heart of enemy territory. (US Navy)

News of a new class of giant Soviet submarines is filtering through to the West, where it has been given the name *Typhoon*. These submarines are some 175m long and powered by two nuclear reactors to give a speed of about 25 knots. One submarine can carry at least 20 SSN-X-20 missiles, each of which contains 9 or possibly 12 individually targeted warheads with a range of 5,000 miles. A double-skinned hull makes the submarine almost impervious to conventional anti-submarine weapons: nuclear depth-charges will probably be necessary to sink it. The nuclear threat to Europe and North America posed by Soviet deployment of this potent weapon, probably in protected areas or under the ice, may well result in significant changes to NATO defence strategy. Two have so far been launched and two, it is reported, are under construction.

51 Lynx about to land on its parent ship. Carried on board British Types 21, 22 and 42 frigates, these helicopters are versatile and can be equipped for anti-submarine classification and attack (A/S torpedoes), air-to-surface search and strike operations (air-to-surface Sea Skua missiles (see plate 66) — mainly intended for use against lightly defended targets such as fast missile attack craft but capable of crippling and even sinking larger targets, as demonstrated in the Falklands campaign in 1982. (Westland Helicopters)

52 Sea King Airborne Early Warning (AEW) helicopter equipped with 'Searchwater' advanced surveillance radar. First embarked in the light aircraft carrier HMS *Illustrious* in 1982, these helicopters will go some way to restoring the dangerous gap caused when carrier-based AEW fixed wing aircraft were discarded because carriers ceased to have catapults. (Westland Helicopters)

Sea King in the ASW (anti-submarine) role carrying four Mk 44 anti-submarine torpedoes. (Westland Helicopters)

Sea King with dunking sonar. A helicopter's ability to move rapidly from one search position to another means a submarine captain cannot predict where the sonar will next be lowered into the water. (Ministry of Defence)

55 A Lynx landing on HMS *Birmingham* demonstrating operational capability in very bad weather conditions. (Ministry of Defence)

56 French Dauphin 365 carrying four AS.15TT anti-ship missiles. This helicopter is primarily designed for attacking enemy warships but it can also be employed for coastal surveillance and for escorting ships. Perhaps its most significant role will be as a link for providing over-the-horizon target information to long-range ship and shore-based missile systems. (Aerospatiale)

French Super-Puma with two Exocet missiles for the anti-ship role. In the anti-submarine role this helicopter can be equipped with two torpedoes and dunking sonar or MAD (magnetic anomaly detection equipment) and sonobuoys. (Aerospatiale)

Seahawk SH-60B on board USS *McInerny* (FFG-8). The helicopter is primarily intended for the US Navy's LAMPS (light airborne multi-purpose systems) which is aimed to extend the reach of surface ships in anti-submarine warfare and in the use of long-range surface-to-surface missile systems. (US Navy)

59 Exocet MM 40 fired from a French warship. This latest mark of the Exocet surface-to-surface missile version with a 165 kg warhead has a range of more than 70 km at high subsonic speed at very low altitude. Terminal guidance is by active radar. (Aerospatiale)

60 Exocet surface-to-surface missile, with a 'fire-and-forget' capability, being fired from HMS *Norfolk*, one of the four British light cruisers to be equipped with four single-cell (no reload) units. (Ministry of Defence)

Anti-submarine MK 44 torpedo dropped by a helicopter. The ship-helicopter combination is an invaluable anti-submarine weapon system but the payload is, of course, limited. (Ministry of Defence)

62 Seadart is a surface-to-air missile system for use against both high and very low flying aircraft. It can also be used as an anti-surface weapon and it has an anti-missile capability. The published range is 'at least 30 km'. (British Aerospace)

63 British Seadart anti-air and anti-surface missiles in their twin launcher. A much lighter system, consisting of a simple deck-mounted box launcher, can be installed in ships from 300 tons upwards enabling the fire-power of a destroyer to be carried on board smaller, less expensive vessels. (Ministry of Defence)

An anti-air and anti-missile Seawolf missile being fired from a new and relatively inexpensive light-weight launcher converted from an earlier Seacat missile launcher. The original GWS 25 self-defence system can only be fitted on board ships of 3000 tons or larger but the new light-weight outfit enables much smaller ships to defend themselves against anti-ship missiles. (British Aerospace)

65 Four Sea Skua anti-ship sea-skimming missiles can be carried by quite small helicopters but the weapon is currently only fitted to the British Lynx shown here. During the Falklands conflict Sea Skuas sank one ship and crippled others in very bad weather conditions and by night. The system gives the attacking ship (which can be small) a trans-horizon capability while maintaining electronic silence. (British Aerospace)

Sea Skua anti-ship missile being launched from Lynx helicopter. (British Aerospace)

67 Test firing of a Polaris strategic ballistic missile from a British SSBN. Now equipped with multiple Chevaline nuclear warheads the 16 missiles carried on board each SSBN have a published range of about 4630 km. They are, of course, fired from the submarine fully submerged. (Ministry of Defence)

Trident fired from USS *Ohio* (see plate 49) in January 1982 during a 'Demonstration and Shakedown Operation' off the coast of Florida. (US Navy)

69 Tomahawk cruise missile after a sub-surface launch off the coast of California, February 1976. Armed with a conventional or nuclear warhead, Tomahawk can be fired from surface ships, submarines, aircraft or mobile ground units. The ship-attack version has a published range of 200 n.m. (*c.* 350 km) and approaches its target in a sea-skimming, evasive flight manoeuvre designed to elude defences and to conceal direction of launch. (US Navy)

) The submarine-launched Harpoon sea-skimming sub-surface to surface anti-ship missile is maintained at the desired height by a radar altimeter and propelled by a turbojet engine out to ranges in excess of 91 km. Terminal guidance is by active radar. It is launched in a capsule (which falls away after breaking the surface) from a standard submarine torpedo tube and gives the attacking submarine a striking range compatible with its long-range sonar and classification capability. (McDonnell Douglas)

1 The anti-ship Harpoon being fired from a canister launch system aboard ship. These missiles can also be launched from aircraft. (McDonnell Douglas)

72 New types of gun, even single mountings like this Mk 8 4.5 inch (114 mm) mounting on a British Type 42 frigate, have given ship-borne gunnery fresh life. Associated with an effective radar system, this single mounting fires 25 rounds per minute accurately out to a maximum range of 22 km. As demonstrated in the Falklands conflict, guns like this also have an important role for shore bombardment. (Vickers Shipbuilding)

73 US guided missile patrol combatant (hydrofoil) *Taurus* in the Pacific in 1981. It is small fast craft of this kind that have given a new lease of life to the old motor torpedo and gun boat concept so valuable in relatively calm or sheltered waters. (US Navy)

'4 Corvus is a quick-reaction window-dispensing rocket system for self defence against air-to-surface and surface-to-surface missiles. The window (chaff) clouds are deployed to surround the ship at a range of about 1 km where they act as 'bait' to incoming hostile missiles. (Vickers Shipbuilding)

75 An Aegis SM2 missile being fired from USS *Norton Sound* in 1977. This new generation surface-to-air weapon will soon form the primary defensive missile system in the US Navy. It is designed to destroy small fast targets (for example, anti-ship cruise missiles) as well as missile-launcher platforms in hostile environments created by weather or countermeasures. The controlling multi-function phased-array radar is high-performance electronically scanned equipment capable of maintaining all-round surveillance while simultaneously detecting and tracking multiple targets. (US Navy)

An RGM 84A Harpoon anti-ship missile launched by USS *Badger* in 1980 on its way to hit a patrol boat target over the horizon. This surface-to-surface variant of the Harpoon missile, which is also seen in sub-surface-to-surface (Subharpoon) and air-to-surface roles, is the US Navy's principal anti-ship weapon and as such is one of the important 'key resources'. (US Navy)

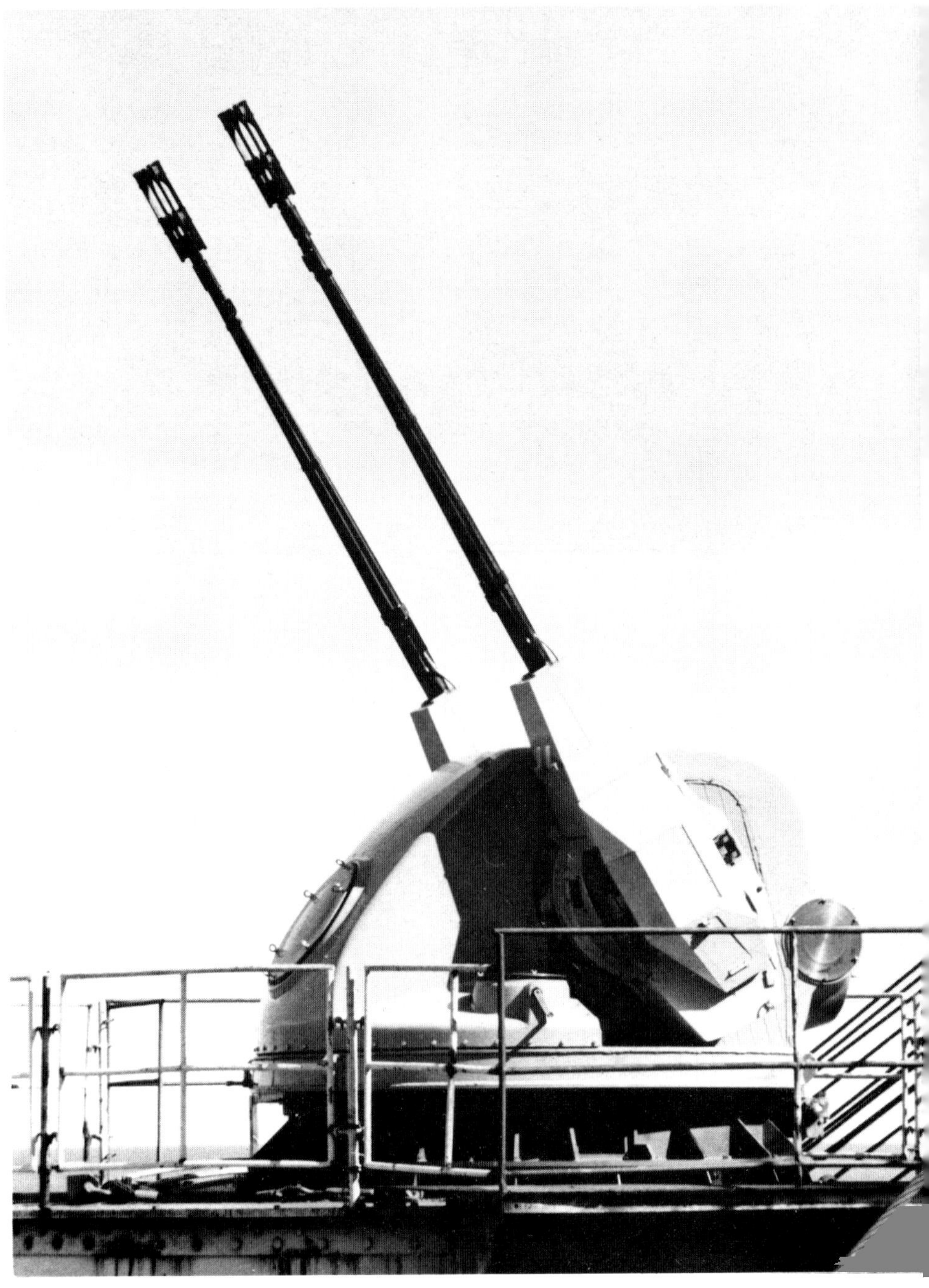

77 The Italian OE/OTO 35 mm twin gun mounting is primarily intended for anti-aircraft and anti-missile point defence with a secondary anti-ship and anti-shore role. The guns themselves are long-proven Oerlikons with a combined rate of fire of 1100 rounds per minute. The comparatively light weight of the mounting means it can be installed in merchant ships of virtually any tonnage as well as naval vessels. When fully loaded it is automatic and unmanned in operation. (Oto Melara)

8 The Italian Otomat sea-skimming anti-ship missile has a range of 60 km with active radar homing giving a high single-shot kill probability: the 210 kg warhead contains 60 kg of explosive. Target information for the system can be supplied from active or passive sources or from external sources via a data link. The launcher-container can be installed quickly and is suitable for small vessels including fast missile attack craft as shown here. (Oto Melara)

9 The Italian Albatro missile launcher for defensive Sea Sparrow or Aspide surface-to-air missiles. (Oto Melara)

80 Tigerfish, the Royal Navy's latest wire-guided submarine torpedo. Designed for attacking fast, deep submarines which might be either noisy or quiet, it has a homing head which can be commanded to adopt a passive or active mode. The weapon also has an anti-ship capability; but it was Mk 8 torpedoes — in service more than 50 years ago — which HMS *Conqueror* used to sink the Argentinian cruiser *General Belgrano*. (Marconi Space and Defence Systems)

81 Although anti-submarine helicopters are more usually used as torpedo vehicles, a Ship-borne Torpedo Weapon System (STWS) of the kind shown here is valuable in certain circumstances. However, its use implies that the attacking ship is within range of the submarine's own weapons. (Plessey Marine)

Part IV

Some Thoughts on the Conduct of Naval Action

How should naval operations be conducted in the new circumstances outlined above? Unfortunately we run up against a methodological problem here, since any answer to the question depends above all on an 'appreciation of the situation' based on hard facts firmly fixed in time and space. But our purpose is not to deal with specific cases but to talk in very general terms. (In particular, it must be emphasized that in no way is the French navy's position singled out.) It is possible only to make some remarks on a few of the choices available to those conducting naval operations.

Bearing in mind the ever-narrowing gap between preparation for action and action itself, we shall start with a brief examination of the choices to be made in advance. We shall then go on to basic choices that have to be made at the start of an operation. Finally, we shall touch briefly on certain operational problems that would probably arise during naval confrontations of any magnitude. Clearly, this division for the simplification of the argument is to some degree artificial, since in reality there would be much interaction between the different stages. Furthermore, the beginning of operations will not necessarily be clear-cut, since it is part of a process involving almost permanent tension. This is another problem to which we shall return.

9

CHOICES TO BE MADE IN ADVANCE

Among the options that have to be selected in advance, there is one that overrides all others: for what kind of confrontation does any given state prepare its navy? The difficulty here is that the answer is not necessarily total war. We have seen, indeed, that a naval operation can take place at several different levels of confrontation which are all allied to the political-strategic situation of the moment in the countries implicated. In this regard, each state is in a particular situation that largely dictates its general policy. This fact ought logically to be interpreted in the naval sphere as an indication of the kind of confrontation for which it should prepare itself. But this simple line of reasoning is very difficult to put into practice because it is extremely rare for a political power to have an aim that is clear and single-minded. The other reason is that technical experts are greatly tempted to demand the best but financiers can rarely satisfy every demand. Besides, situations often develop very quickly, while a navy can only develop slowly.

If all the countries faced with these difficulties are considered, two simple cases can be identified: that of the largest nations who are in the comfortable situation of being able to prepare for anything; and that of the very small nations whose aims can only be very limited. In point of fact, many countries are in a intermediate situation where they certainly cannot be prepared for all events but where they have, all the same, enough resources to have options to choose from. It is for these nations, then, that the problems are greatest. The most obvious mistake is to define the naval forces of such a state as a scaled-down version of a very large navy, since the smaller navy is almost bound to lack both political purpose and technical coherence.

A search for the best option starts with an overall military policy conforming to a firm general policy; and it goes on to define the naval component of this military policy as a function of the nation's geo-strategic, economic, technical and industrial position. The right solution is only arrived at by dialogue and continual reassessment. However that may be, if the first choice to make beforehand is clearly perceived, it should give a general indication of the kind of confrontation to expect. All this is primarily a political affair. Naval experts will have a greater share when the characteristics of naval confrontations are defined.

What, then, are the characteristics of the confrontations for which preparations must be made? In this respect, the choice of options will, at any given moment, already have been made, so that it will have every appearance of being commonplace. The fact that the selected option has an air of permanence about it makes one forget that it is decisive and one can even lose clear sight of it altogether. The analyses of the preceding chapters act as a guide to the kind of features of confrontations that can be contemplated.

The level of intensity is certainly the most striking single feature. The lowest level, low tension, is almost straightforward and it is this that dictates the mainstream capabilities of all navies. The ability to deal with the state of continual crisis in which we live is rather less straightforward. We pointed out in part III that this situation already poses problems of intelligence gathering, communications and command. In every case it depends on choices connected with other characteristics (which we will discuss further on), and in particular with the all-important geographical feature of location.

Preparedness for limited war involves a series of very complex options because, even when limited, naval warfare can assume widely diverse forms and attain very varied levels of intensity. The choice of options will largely be dictated by the threat to which the country concerned reckons it is subject and which will demand capabilities of a varying degree of sophistication. For all that, this is the level of intensity for which many states can still claim to equip their navies.

Fitness for total war or even a serious nuclear crisis is more selective because it supposes that the country concerned is capable of attaining the highest quality in at least one notable and coherent aspect of the 'key resources'. Of course, an evaluation of the probability of such a major confrontation's occurring plays a part here. But, if the probability is judged to be low, its part as one of the deciding factors is limited by the necessity of ensuring the credibility of forces at all levels, in order to safeguard the deterrent concept to which the state concerned will probably be attached. Conversely, an ambitious state which is looking for a crack in the enemy's deterrent apparatus and does not completely exclude the notion of direct attack will very carefully examine the possibilities afforded at this level of intensity.

But it is rare for a country seeking a coherent naval policy to discuss the matter as if it depended on itself alone. In practice, all countries have relations of friendship, potential hostility or indifference with other countries and these relations are ratified by various pacts, treaties and agreements. These are clearly a prime factor in the preliminary political choices to be made. However, one of the constraints engendered by the technical developments examined in part III, and in particular by the advent of data processing in methods of communication and command, is that the operational co-operation at sea that should logically result from the application of such mutual agreements necessitates a technical compatability that cannot be improvised. Although technical ingenuity may offer solutions to this kind of difficulty, account has still to be taken of them in time, and the price paid. In short, this is an area where policy is impeded by technical factors and where scientists and designers are always impatient to know the decisions of the policy makers. It is also, considered world-wide, an area where arms sales can have a remarkable effect on political options, and vice versa.

One of the first important decisions to be made is whether one should aim to operate at a distance or only in one's own home waters and approaches. Of course, only the choice of being able to operate at long range allows all threats to be catered for, particularly those that might bear on maritime transport, which is always more or less world-wide, or on remote commercial and political interests. Long-range operations demand considerable resources — combat units, reliable communications and logistic support. They also raise the question of overseas bases. It is true that the latter can, to a considerable extent, be replaced by mobile support ships; but these often require calm, sheltered waters, are costly, and do not provide for crews' need for relaxation. So it is still desirable to arrange for shore facilities overseas, though these need not necessarily be unilateral political possessions. All this must be taken into account in any coherent foreign policy. Finally, it must be emphasized that when seeking to extend a navy's capabilities overseas, there is a risk of confusing the ability to sustain a presence at long range during a period of tension with actually making war at the same distance: war creates a completely different situation with regard to the consumption of fuel and munitions, the exigencies of reliable communications, the requirements of maintenance and repair and lastly the scale of crews' medical needs. So far as continuing resources are concerned, wartime ambitions can, then, only be more modest than those during a time of ordinary tension.

The next important but thorny problem is whether to prepare for a long or a short operation. Our analysis of the possibilities for naval confrontation tends to show that the likelihood of a long, or fairly long, operation cannot be dismissed. Moreover, it must be emphasized that during a period of serious tension, or during any of the intermediate situations envisaged, navies' activities will probably last much longer than those of the other armed forces, since a navy will almost certainly be involved in a crisis sooner and stay involved for longer; and, anyway, at sea one cannot simply stop engines and wait! In other words, it seems that today, as formerly, a navy that wants to be ready to face a wide range of eventualities including war itself must provision and organize itself for operations which might last for several months. It must also be able to hold out in situations of tension and crisis; and one can easily imagine these lasting for years.

Finally, any country must obviously decide clearly and well in advance what methods of co-operation must be made available between the different forces of that country. Co-operation involves not only the armed forces themselves but also the whole defence structure, if the sharp end is to be properly supported from the rear and all the needs satisfied. Policy agreements in this area are by no means easy to achieve.

Having defined the operational features that must be prepared for, the next step is to work out the fundamental requirements of a naval arm. This is the whole problem of genetic strategy which occupies staff planners constantly; and there is no question here of presenting them with an overall solution. We must, however, consider the possible systems of forces and the criteria for choosing between them, the use to which geographical resources should be put and the part that the choice of weapons systems should play.

Turning first to the choices of systems of forces, the developments we have analysed do not appear to change the fundamental principles of this very old question, which is the classical basis of all staff work. It is a matter of starting with the capabilities one wants to possess when dealing with territories, commercial assets at sea and forces, as a function of the operations one wants to put in train, and then of translating these considerations into coherent bodies of military resources constituting systems of forces and of logistic support. Three points can be emphasized. The first is traditional at sea: it concerns the aptitude for endurance, always indispensable, whether in peacetime, periods of tension, crisis or war itself. The two others, which are still evolving, are already imposing considerable constraints, as has been noted in part III with regard to their technical aspects. The diversity of desirable resources has greatly increased and can provide for the needs of even a well-defined type of confrontation. In addition, the volume of a system that is capable of remaining coherent in total war has become much greater; this is the case with what we have called the elementary naval unit.

These developments do not make choices easy for small or medium-sized navies, particularly if they are keen to play their full role in total war. However, there is a different approach which a political power might adopt when looking for a solution to this problem. By their nature, many of the new resources that have figured in our inventory technically lend themselves to co-operation and to a sharing of the products. It is rather difficult to share the services of a warship, of course; but it is a great deal easier, in principle, to share those of a reconnaissance satellite, a ground-array sonar network, a computer facility or modern aids to navigation.

Turning to the role played by geographical resources in the conceiving of and preparation for naval warfare, this is clearly important to the choice of systems; and, as we have seen, technical developments are bringing about important material innovations in this respect. Before the last war, major naval ports were defended by powerful gun batteries or by other fixed defences. Then, during the war, amphibious operations and landings, together with the development of airborne troops who could circumnavigate this kind of defence, and various other weapons, rendered fortifications obsolete because their immobility and the modest range of their weapons made it all too easy to concentrate all means against them. On the whole, cases where land emplacements could intervene in naval warfare were rare; and they have now largely disappeared, at least in those countries where a possible naval enemy is not operating in the immediate vicinity.

With the appearance of missiles — and part III has shown how many and varied are the perspectives that they open, or could open in association with modern methods of search and location, particularly if missiles acquired the ability to relocate and identify their target — it is now entirely conceivable that missiles might comprise a new kind of coastal artillery capable of engaging surface vessels at sea out to a considerable range. It would seem, therefore, that the question of coastal defence systems should be reintroduced into naval thinking.

Another means of warfare that might take on a new lease of life with the advent of missiles (mentioned in part III) is the small surface ship or fast attack craft. Missiles can give such craft a level of fire power and a range of engagement that were certainly not available to them with guns or torpedoes. It is true that small craft are still handicapped in the open seas in bad weather and are vulnerable to attack by naval aircraft; but there are plenty of areas in the world that are sheltered by geography and that offer nearby hiding-places from enemy aircraft. In any case, small craft expose themselves to air reconnaissance for comparatively short periods in these confined waters where large ships have restricted room for manoeuvre. The areas where fast attack craft can best operate quite often possess great strategic significance, notably in places where an important strategic zone coincides with a dense archipelago or a heavily indented coastline. Examples can be found in the Aegean Sea, the Straits of Denmark, the Malaccan Straits and the northern Norwegian fjords. When supported by such geographical facilities, fast missile-attack craft could be extremely formidable.

New possibilities connected with geography are also appearing in mine warfare. These possibilities relate not only to the development of mines themselves but still more, as suggested previously, to the new concept of using mines offensively. Offensive mine warfare could come to be used extensively in suitable sea lanes leading to enemy territory.

Returning to the idea of fixed acoustic ground arrays for the detection of submarines, naval warfare could increasingly be influenced by geographical considerations if the operational effectiveness of fixed arrays is proved. Obviously they are likely to be really effective only in certain favourable positions — at points of passage which cannot be avoided or where navigable water is constricted in some way. Fixed arrays are bound to be less profitable in the open sea but, even here, they could modify the geographical framework of future battles; for example, the zones which they cover could become sanctuaries for certain vulnerable operations, such as the assembly or dispersal of convoys and the sailing or return of SSBNs; or they could even play a part in ASW operations.

The possibility of a new kind of coastal artillery, the employment of fast missile-attack craft in favourable areas, offensive mining where the enemy is most vulnerable and establishing areas guarded by listening arrays — all offer, then, some interesting food for thought at the stage of analysing what naval tools are required.

The third theme for discussion is the choice of means for actual fighting. Today it seems that we must think in terms of weapons systems rather than the naval units that carry them, despite the habit of describing them by the ships in which they are carried. Indeed, because we are not in any way concerned with plans for any particular navy, it would anyway seem more fruitful to base our research on weapons systems in the broadest sense. In many cases it is the weapons more than the weapon carriers that would distinguish future battles. In many cases too it is the weapons system that dictates the architecture of the carrier and not the other way round. We have already noted that weapons systems are sometimes independent of their carriers.

However, this is a highly technical and enormous area, and it would be presumptuous either to claim that we can examine here everything that is being done or being prepared in this field, or, above all, to attempt some kind of judgement. Nevertheless it may be possible to isolate some ideas for guidance on the subject of systems that can be envisaged by considering these from the standpoint of both the type of confrontation and the type of fighting the systems will serve.

The first point is that the importance of search and reconnaissance — which has always been great by reason of the fundamental uncertainty, in a maritime environment, about an enemy's position — will assume new dimensions with the arrival of reconnaissance satellites and fixed listening arrays. It is vital, for the success of all kinds of naval operations and engagements, to be thoroughly well informed about the enemy both when studying his strategic deployment and when preparing for action. It is not yet proven, of course, that the new systems have attained a state of full operational efficiency. But navies that want to be of significance should certainly give high priority to being well informed about these projects with a view to acquiring at least some of these systems and take pains to avoid a possible enemy's learning anything about the technology involved.

There is another side to this coin. It is essential, from an operational point of view, to know what the enemy has been able to observe and learn about one's own forces. In the future many things will have to be considered in terms of both one's own frequency of transit through a given area and the discriminatory powers of the enemy's means of observation.

If the possession of patrol aircraft already marks an important step in naval capabilities, it is certain that reconnaissance satellites will mark a new threshold which will be still more selective. Satellites, are, of course, a costly means of search but it has already been pointed out that they lend themselves well to being used in common with several countries. Furthermore, naval reconnaissance does not necessarily demand heavy, manoeuvrable and short-lived satellites: a passive detection satellite, fairly light and with a long life, would be able to provide invaluable strategic information in war and would be a good deal less expensive.

The second indispensable field of warfare, directly born of modern technology, is that of electronic warfare and now what might be called acoustic warfare. However, the application of these sophisticated techniques will probably be less universal than the use of satellites because in certain limited confrontations the comparatively low-level technology available to the belligerents would leave little place for such sophisticated methods. On the other hand, the role of electronic and acoustic warfare will undoubtedly assume increasing importance in a serious crisis and in the preliminary skirmishing or the prolongation of war itself; and they will be integrated more and more into all kinds of operations besides becoming inseparable from developments in micro-processing which has, among other virtues, the very rare quality of becoming less expensive with the passage of time.

Technical developments for search will gradually cause the need for electronic silence to decrease (satellites can *see*) and may have to give way, to some extent, to the various kinds of deception which merit very careful consideration not only in the final stages of an engagement when missiles are winging their way towards their targets but from the moment of relocation and even during the search stage. There will also have to be improvements in jamming and decoying methods because these can extend the means of action in situations where neutralization rather than destruction of some actor on the naval stage is sought.

These remarks on search and electronic warfare are applicable to a wide range of choices of naval policy because the systems can be used in almost every kind of operation. The next area to be examined is certainly crucial but at the same time more limited because it only concerns countries that want to play a part in total war, if only in the deterrent role. This, of course, is the capacity for nuclear combat — which entails giving all, or most, weapons systems a nuclear capability. One must obviously talk of systems in their broadest sense because the combatants will be as much concerned with nuclear protection as with actual nuclear weapons. It is clear how much this choice can depend on the numerous technical options available; but to those of us who advocate deterrence it seems to be the essential condition for credibility and for eventual success in the circumstances created by the existence of nuclear weapons.

What, then, must a package of nuclear weapons consist of? The fact that a target at sea is by definition mobile means that there is always a degree of uncertainty about its future position, and from this results the necessity of giving naval nuclear weapons sufficient power. However, it would be futile to hope to destroy an entire naval force at a single blow; a nuclear weapon that could eliminate a large force would almost certainly harm the attacker himself. An explosive power equivalent to a few hundred kilotonnes of TNT would be sufficient. To be effective against a submarine, a nuclear explosion must take place underwater. This would, of course, also be detrimental to the attacker, who would have to continue the battle in contaminated water, and, indeed, the whole marine environment would be affected. Nuclear air-bursts are preferable against surface vessels, partly for reasons already given but also in order to facilitate co-operation with friendly submarines. It is, however, necessary to have weapons that can be exploded at the precise height required.

We must now turn to the element that pervades the entire naval panoply — the missile. We have seen that missiles are almost everywhere and could come from almost anywhere. So the question is how best to mount defences against them. It is clearly tempting to think first of attacking the missile launcher because the destruction of a launcher obviously includes its weapons and creates, at least for a while, a sector without a missile threat. This will quite often be feasible provided that widely diverse and effective means are available for use against aircraft, surface vessels, submarines and even shore installations — though these last involve a problem of principle to which we shall return. The first option in face of a missile threat is therefore to concentrate on engaging the launchers, a choice that involves a huge 'elementary naval unit' and is therefore costly. Moreover, it is unlikely, in view of the variety and universality of missiles, that this action would in itself guarantee total security. Effective anti-missile systems appear, therefore, to be indispensable to anybody who wants to be able to participate in a war that is not very limited, particularly if numerous and powerful 'elementary naval units' are not available.

Something else has to be said about an anti-ship missile when its payload is non-nuclear. Present-day anti-ship missiles do not reach the vital area of a target — that is, that part of a ship which is below the waterline (a non-vital area is that part of a ship which is above the waterline). Taking into account the enormous amount of fighting equipment carried in the upper part of a ship, a missile hit will certainly deprive it of the ability to fight. But it is not likely to sink a ship and, assuming that the crew is fully trained in damage-control procedures, it should be able to keep under way and it will probably regain its base. In a short war, this is not a serious drawback for the enemy because he can reckon on the ship's not being able to recover its operational capabilities before the end of the war. But, as we have seen, it would be unwise to dismiss all thoughts of a long war. If, furthermore, the target is a merchant vessel, a missile attack that does not prevent it from arriving back in port must be counted as a failure.

Therefore it is probably wise, when striving for an all-round effective capability, to acquire the means to sink an enemy, whether by missiles capable of reaching vital areas or by using, as a follow-up, other weapons capable of sinking a ship whose upper works are already damaged. Furthermore, it could be tactically disadvantageous to limit one's threat to a single kind of weapon, since one would run the risk of simplifying an enemy's defensive problems.

Before leaving the subject of missiles, it is worth looking at a variant which could prove very useful for adapting a naval tool to possible changes in its ability to deal with confrontations. Missile systems can now be containerized or mounted in prefabricated shelters which can be installed very quickly on a hastily fitted-out carrier. The advantages are obvious and the concept seems to be entirely practicable.

A final question concerning weapons systems is whether to choose active or passive detection methods. The answer, quite simply, is that it is hard to see how one can avoid having both.

An enemy who has staked everything on only one of the two methods can easily be outwitted, but a unit with both systems can exploit any given situation to the best advantage, particularly where a force's appropriate unit functions have been intelligently apportioned. The navy with only one of the two possibilities is, in fact, outclassed by the navy with both.

In this brief survey of the choices a navy has to make in advance which will dictate the conduct of future operations, we have seen the necessity of being quite clear about the kind of operations in which one wishes to be able to take an active part, in the context of other navies' capabilities, while emphasizing the need for endurance at sea during a crisis and for inter-service co-ordination. While underlining the very broad scale of systems required by a force, we suggested that the solution may lie in co-operating with other friendly countries. Then we looked at the part that geography can play in naval warfare, especially with regard to a new kind of coastal artillery, fast missile-attack craft, fixed acoustic ground arrays and offensive mining. Then, while still studying the naval arm, we commented on several aspects of weapons systems — their growing significance in comparison with their carriers, the extreme importance of new techniques for search, the omnipresence of electronic and acoustic warfare, the importance of having a capacity for nuclear fighting, the need for anti-missile systems and for having anti-ship missiles capable of actually sinking ships and, finally, so far as detection goes, the importance of not staking everything on either an active or a passive system.

10

BASIC OPTIONS AT THE START OF OPERATIONS

A clear distinction must be made here between naval operations at a level below that of serious crisis and those at a higher level. Operations during a state of tension or continual crisis are peculiar in that for more than 30 years a number of navies have been practising them while others have been able to observe them to a considerable extent. This is therefore a subject about which a great deal is known; and technological developments concerned with operations at this level should not spring too many surprises. However, this does not lessen the fact that such operations still necessitate a positive choice of options.

These options are primarily concerned with logistics, because only a sound logistical choice will meet the needs of these operations, which are generally long. But choosing the right organization for command and control is almost equally important; and here loyalty to the political aim is paramount. But logistics and organization of command are to some extent preliminaries to the main point at issue: the question of choosing what kind of pressure to exercise on the forces one is confronted with. Since it is not a case of actual war, it is certainly not a matter of destroying the enemy forces. It can be assumed that the political power will strictly forbid that at this stage. Nevertheless, some way must be found of imposing one's will or thwarting the will of one's opponent. The power must behave in such a way as to intimidate or show that it is not itself intimidated. In this respect, navies generally enjoy a certain imaginative latitude in the way they go about their business;

and this stems from long tradition. The options concern the level of aggressiveness to choose and the degree of risk of aggravation that can be accepted in terms of political priorities. Sometimes it is sufficient simply to be seen at the right place at the right time.

Of course, the optimum result is to influence the enemy to such an extent that the political objectives are achieved without recourse to the level of intensity which is war. If such is not the case and if, in the end, it is necessary to push a trial of strength up to the point of open hostilities, a new situation opens up with consequent new options to choose from. Unfortunately, one comes up against a methodological difficulty here because we do not know in what conditions this passage from serious crisis to war will be effected: we do not yet have enough solid data to work on at this stage in our debate. Although a concrete appraisal of the situation therefore cannot be made, this general inquiry can none the less provide certain elements for an evaluation, even if there are necessarily some gaps.

With this reservation, we can say that it seems appropriate to treat the case of serious crisis and the case of war as one, because probably one can successfully tackle a serious crisis only if a clear view of the war that could follow is in the minds of all those responsible, even (and perhaps above all) if the aim is to avoid war. If it is agreed that in a serious crisis the choices relating to logistics, organization, command and behaviour will always be supremely important, the fresh options which present themselves will be closely related to those of war, even if they fall short of the brink during the process of confrontation.

We therefore propose to review some of the constant principles for the conduct of naval operations — the principles of war, in fact — and then inquire into the respective merits of offensive and defensive attitudes. We shall then consider whether it is advisable to attack first the enemy's forces, or his commercial assets at sea or his territories. Certain abiding principles must be kept in mind. To begin with, various means of warfare are intended for either destroying, capturing or neutralizing an enemy. The ability of a naval force to destroy has vastly increased; its ability to capture, on the other hand, has scarcely improved; but its ability to neutralize the enemy has, as we have seen, encountered new possibilities with the development of electronic warfare.

Secondly in naval warfare as in any show of force, one must obviously strive to make the best use of any trump cards that have been dealt; to minimize any of one's own weaknesses; and to exploit the imbalances that almost always exist between enemies with regard to the geographical situation, local vulnerability, military potential and, indeed, the political situation itself.

Thirdly it is as indispensable as ever today to practise a sensible economy of effort; to keep a close watch on maintaining one's own freedom of action; and to achieve the concentration of force that is necessary for attacking or defending oneself effectively.

Having said that, should one take the offensive or remain on the defensive? In some situations, of course, the question answers itself. For example, if one takes the initiative for a distant, limited war calling for the transportation and disembarkation of an expeditionary force, then *ipso facto* one is taking the offensive position. The question does arise, however, in the naval arena, in the majority of cases where one has not taken a major naval initiative oneself. In particular, it arises when, during total war, one is in a globally defensive position as a result of fundamental political choices. Nevertheless, an offensive at sea does not have the same political significance as one on land, particularly if it respects enemy territorial waters; it remains an available choice, albeit with certain limitations to which we shall return. In any case, the choice between offence and defence will in practice undoubtedly be heavily influenced by political considerations that lie entirely with governments. We shall thus be content with examining the strictly military aspects.

The choice is largely dictated by the general strategic situation and the circumstances at the time. In the first place, it depends upon the relative strengths of one's own and the enemy's forces: obviously it would not make much sense to instigate a wholehearted offensive against an enemy much more powerful than oneself. It is assumed, for the sake of argument, that this will not happen.

The choice also depends upon the enemy's general position and, in particular, on his deployment. It is, in fact, his deployment that suggests whether it is possible to achieve the necessary concentration against him or whether there is a danger of his robbing one's own forces of their freedom of action. On the other hand, if the enemy has not deployed, if he is not free to manoeuvre, and if he has been deprived of one part of his means of action, the moment is favourable, in principle at least, for an attack so as to destroy him or at least to inflict severe losses and take the dominant position.

Geography too is a critical factor in choosing the right option because it can introduce interesting points of imbalance. It is especially relevant in a conflict between a naval power with easy access to the open seas and a continental power in the reverse situation; the interests of the first will generally be to aggravate the enemy's handicap as soon as possible by attacking him so as to prevent his gaining the open ocean. In all this, however, the limitations mentioned earlier apply. These arise from the constraints that an intelligent application of deterrent strategy can impose if, at the time when the choice of options seems open for attack or defence, a nuclear exchange reaching national territories has not begun. If the naval attack envisaged is directed at enemy territory, is it acceptable at this stage? This must be for the political power to decide; but the naval command can offer suggestions with regard to the conduct of operations, and these will be discussed later.

Another potentially decisive imbalance is that of vulnerability. One immediately thinks of one country's dependence on maritime transport in comparison with another. If one of the belligerents has an Achilles' heel in this respect, it would in principle be in his enemy's interests to exploit the situation as quickly as possible by taking the offensive. But there are other considerations here regarding the choice to be made about the main aims of an offensive.

Although the choice between offence and defence depends largely upon the above factors, it is none the less not of a uniform nature: to take the offensive against submarines, against surface forces, against aircraft, against bases or against assets at sea involves, in fact, quite distinct and separate choices and problems.

To take the offensive against submarines is not as simple as it may appear. Either they are in their home ports and one comes up against the problem of an attack on bases if it is the beginning of a total war; or else they are at sea where their positions can be known only approximately. There is, however, one case that favours an offensive against submarines: where geography imposes more or less permanent restrictions on passage, submarines can be attacked in transit.

An offensive against surface forces is much easier to imagine and will become more and more practicable with developments in search and surveillance. Moreover, in the open sea, such an offensive should not meet with any political obstacle. With regard to aircraft, there are two possible situations: they may be on board ships where they are subject to the same considerations as surface forces; or they may be land-based, and one is again faced with the problem of attacking the bases if one wishes to take the offensive. An attack on merchant shipping and other enemy assets at sea is relatively easy to undertake, but it poses a considerable problem in terms of effectiveness.

This leads us to the second series of options: should one tackle forces, commercial interests at sea or territories? This question constantly preoccupies naval historians seeking lessons with a universal message, but their suggested answers are often based on examples or arguments drawn from Franco-British wars of the past — that is, from particular and not general situations. In fact, it is impossible to give a reply that will always be valid, other than by saying, of course, that if one *can* eliminate an enemy's naval forces one could afterwards dispose of his seaborne commerce and that this, therefore, is an advantageous option to choose. So far as enterprises against territories are concerned, we have seen that by far the most damaging is nuclear bombardment at long range; and this is possible even without the enemy forces having first been neutralized.

The choice therefore depends, at the end of the day, on an appreciation of the situation based on the factors governing the conflict in question. Some general observations apply to most situations. The problem of attacking a territory has assumed today a completely new dimension which we have reviewed with regard to the nuclear factor. If it is a matter of total war, the biggest question concerns the use of nuclear weapons. For a power that seeks deterrence or is subject to deterrence as a fact of life, the decision to use nuclear weapons carried by ships or submarines against an enemy territory is not a question of naval warfare but of general strategy. The question does not, however, have a simple or unique answer. A nation attached to pure deterrence, based on the threat of anti-city reprisals in response to any major act of aggression, will logically be led to reserve its nuclear-strike capability for use in the eventuality of such an act; but a country or an alliance attracted to a graduated-response strategy starting with anti-military nuclear strikes, or to a strategy that includes commonplace usage of nuclear weapons, will, on the other hand, have a more varied range of options, particularly if the enemy has already broken the state of 'nuclear virginity'. This could be one of those periods at the start of a total war which we envisaged earlier, where an attack on enemy territory with nuclear weapons carried by naval vessels could become a naval question in so far as, whatever the ultimate strategic implications might be, anti-military acts must be militarily optimized. This would create a possible loophole for attacks on bases: the most attractive targets would be submarine bases because the periods submarines spend in harbour are the only times in their operational cycle when one can be sure of finding them in a definitely known position.

If it is not total war, the choices are obviously wider because no point of principle will prohibit an attack upon territories. On the other hand, the means of attack available will have nothing like the destructive power of nuclear weapons, which are by definition excluded. One will therefore resort to conventional attacks or to amphibious landings; and the opportunity for these will clearly depend upon an appreciation of the situation at the time.

Concerning the choice of priorities accorded to attacking commercial shipping or to attacking naval forces, it has to be asked first whether there really is a choice: in order to attack a force, as we have already said, the relative strengths of one's own and enemy forces must be acceptable; and in order to attack assets the means available must be adequate for the purpose. If there really is a choice, it would seem to be based mainly on considerations relating to the kind of war involved and to the anticipated time-scale, and must take into account the fact that attacks on commerce at sea can in any case only *slowly* produce significant military or political results and then only if the attacks are focused on a genuinely serious vulnerability.

At first sight, then, attacking commercial assets at sea is not the choice to make in the expectation of a short war intended to be waged with all available means. However, presented in this way, the analysis applies only to pure assets — merchant ships in the main — and not to military transports supplying the battle; destruction of the latter can, on the contrary, bring about rapid results, and such assets must be treated as naval forces. But, while reflecting on types of warfare in general, we have imagined a kind of long but limited war which could occur as a preliminary to, or as a prolongation of, total war; it could even be chosen deliberately in order to impose severe constraints on an enemy possessing nuclear weapons without taking the risk of provoking strategic reprisals; or it could take place between non-nuclear powers. In such situations the options are wide open and an attack on commercial interests could well be considered, again on condition that their destruction would have serious consequences. In a situation where one is oneself vulnerable in respect of one's own commercial interests at sea and the enemy is not, however, it would appear to be imperative to attack his forces. It is clear, though, that the application of such an idea is not simple.

We conclude these remarks on the choice of attacking forces, commercial interests or land territories by recalling that the final outcome of a war is decided *on land* because life and power are on land. Naval action must therefore be evaluated in terms of the effect it will have on land if it is to achieve one of the goals outlined in part I. This clearly does not prevent a war's decisive turning-point from being a naval action; but it will be decisive only through having allowed a conclusion on land. This, moreover, is one of the reasons why the nuclear factor can be seen as a naval revolution. It gives the naval arm the means whereby it can itself contribute decisively to an attack against land.

11

PROBLEMS OF NAVAL OPERATIONS

To conduct a naval operation is a concrete task that has to be carried out from day to day on the basis of immediate operational intelligence gathered about the enemy, the means at one's disposal and the tactics in force. We have shown, in the course of discussing the general characteristics of naval action, why it is impossible to formulate detailed plans for operations in advance.

On the other hand, the preliminary choices about the kind of war for which one wants to prepare, the requisite naval tools, the offensive or defensive attitudes to adopt and the target priorities would greatly affect the conduct of subsequent operations. It is also highly probable that a state of war would have been preceded by a state of crisis whose effects on the protagonists and on the initial situation would be far from negligible. So one may almost wonder whether there remains, in a survey of this kind, a place for examination of the conduct of operations between the initial situation, the preliminary choices we have discussed, and day-to-day actions that we neither want nor are able to tackle here.

In fact, though, there is a channel, which is no doubt narrow but none the less navigable, through which speculation can lead to some usable pointers without being so general as to be mundane. This belief is based on the idea that, whatever the preliminary choices may be, a certain number of operational problems will be raised because they concern the very nature of naval action. Their proportions, their priorities and their quantifiable factors will vary according to the conflict in question and according to the choices made at an earlier stage; but they are constituents which will always be present. These constituents themselves give rise, at the level of operational strategy, to a number of questions which one can attempt to answer, if only tentatively, and that is what we shall try to do. The list of constituents could be enormously long, but we shall limit it to six questions:

1 What surveillance policy should be adopted?
2 How should SSBNs be operated (if one has them)?
3 How should naval forces be deployed?
4 How should the problem of attacking or defending commercial interests at sea be dealt with?
5 How can action be brought against naval forces?
6 How should mine warfare be conducted?

Firstly, we shall examine the question of search and reconnaissance. We have already emphasized the importance of this function as a necessary preliminary to naval action and noted the wide variety of methods it can include, ranging from common surveillance vessels to patrol aircraft with a great radius of action, and even satellite systems. To expand on this, we can say that other than in exceptional cases, one will not be starting from zero. Continuous plotting of enemy activities in peace and in crisis, the utilization of external intelligence sources both national and foreign, previous studies of the enemy and geographical peculiarities will all normally have allowed one to make an initial estimate of the situation. A state of war will simplify certain matters. Merchant shipping will be taken in hand by the belligerents on each side, and one will have knowledge of, and possibly control over, the movements of friendly vessels. The steps the enemy will take on behalf of his own ships will facilitate identification; passenger cruise-ships will disappear, as will, quite probably, part of the fishing fleet.

A strict economy of force will be as indispensable for search as for other matters, because there will never be enough means to do everything. Priorities must be established with regard to the essential options on the one hand and evaluating the threat on the other. One of the merits of permanent surveillance systems like satellites or fixed ground arrays is that once in position they raise no problems of refuelling or relief on station.

Moreover, surveillance is a principal area for exercising the capacity for endurance, the significance of which we have emphasized several times. Finally, it is vital to know what the enemy knows about *you*, so that efforts can be made to inhibit detection or mislead him, and also so that his probable reactions can be predicted. In this connection, once enemy satellites have been observed, if they are not manoeuvrable one can predict their exact movements by calculating them according to the laws of astronomy. This is a notion to which we shall return when discussing battle.

After the universal preliminary of surveillance, a major operational problem will be that of how to operate SSBNs, at least for those navies that have them. For these the question is of prime importance because SSBNs will be the pivot of the whole conduct of warfare, and their presence at sea leaves nobody indifferent to them. The principle of operating them rests upon two main points: their threat must be mounted with the highest degree of continuity possible at a level fixed by the political authority; and their freedom of action must be ensured. The first point is satisfied by placing in patrol zones, within range of their targets, as many submarines as the political authority will have selected as its compromise between continuity and the scale of the threat to be mounted. Considered in isolation, this is more a technical than an operational problem. The second point, by contrast, is entirely operational; and, in the rather prospective view that we are taking, it is particularly important. Although the main attributes of an SSBN in respect of undetectability, manoeuvrability, reserve of speed and decoy systems allow it virtually unrestricted freedom of action today, the developments we have discussed with regard to attack-type submarines may prevent the SSBN from enjoying anything like so much freedom in the future.

Thus the policy for operating SSBNs must be looked at in new terms, and in relation to whatever new operational means might be afforded to them in the future. The most obvious of these means is an increase in the range of their strategic missiles, which would allow the possible launching areas to be changed at will and would thereby offer a range of operational choices that could be adapted to the enemy's supposed capabilities. But if ever submarines lost their ability to remain hidden and discreet, they would still be highly mobile and well able to defend themselves. SSBN operations would then become a strictly operational problem, manifested by the kind of supporting battle that was suggested earlier when we discussed the changes in submarine capabilities. One conclusion, however, which seemed to emerge from our study of technical developments was that it would probably be an advantage to join battle in a geographical zone where one had established some aids for detecting and locating an enemy.

Having ensured the safety of SSBNs or at least begun to do so, the naval command must decide at the start of hostilities or, better still, before the war is declared, when, where and how to deploy its forces. We have seen that naval action, typically, leaves this question open. Although this problem overlaps that of protecting commercial interests and also that of actual battle, it would seem to have some features all of its own. As with some of the other options we have already examined, there are situations where the answers seem simple — where it is a matter of putting into effect a precise operation on which one takes the initiative. The main pivot of action is obvious here; it only remains to distribute the resources among the different tasks, taking care to achieve economy of effort and to ensure freedom of action for the forces assigned to the principal operation. This is a situation that will obtain mainly in various cases of limited war.

The most difficult and complex case is when, faced by a powerful enemy who has sufficient means to take the initiative in several spheres of action at the same time, one is oneself in a generally defensive posture with only limited means. First of all, the main preliminary choices already made indicate certain directions to follow, above all if they imply initiative. Such a situation anyway imposes on naval forces a certain number of military tasks that, if they are not already under way, must be undertaken immediately because of the crisis: the security of SSBNs and of seaward approaches must be ensured, and measures must be taken to protect trade routes and other interests at sea. These tasks will necessitate the use of resources, the methods of deployment of which will be determined by geographical and material circumstances.

Certain precautions are enjoined by good sense and a

knowledge of the possibilities afforded to an enemy with modern armaments. One must leave at a port only whatever units are absolutely obliged to stay there, since concentration of ships in harbour constitutes a far too vulnerable target which may lead the enemy to reckon that circumstances are favourable for an anti-force strike if he has the means. One must also remain mobile in order to make an appreciation of one's forces by the enemy difficult and to maintain his uncertainty about one's intentions, even if he has means of gaining intelligence about the current situation. One must, as far as possible, arrange one's potential so as to be capable of endurance, above all if the operations follow a crisis.

Whatever deployment is selected obviously depends on that of the enemy as well as on the precise details that intelligence gathered about him could offer concerning the threat he poses. That is why it is impossible to determine one's deployment in advance.

These various considerations will probably have led by themselves to the deployment of all available resources. But if resources remain that have not been assigned to a specific task, and if circumstances allow some margin for manoeuvre, one might consider how to operate and position what was formerly a battle fleet and what might now be called the principal fighting force. First of all, though, is a principal fighting force necessary? That clearly depends on the major preliminary decisions as well as on the enemy's potential. An obvious case is where one of the preliminary choices is to attack enemy territories with carrier-borne aircraft. It goes without saying that the main body must then be composed of attack aircraft-carriers with all the essential support discussed earlier. ASW, air and surface protection units will, with the main body, certainly make up a powerful formation, and this will be a principal fighting force. It will be multi-purpose because it must necessarily consist of almost every type of resource in existence, including SSNs. Such a force would clearly be capable of engaging enemy air or surface forces, or attacking commercial assets at sea. Conversely, if the enemy had a force of this kind, a similar force would then be constituted, so that one would be able either to attack it deliberately or to oppose it.

A principal fighting force could, as suggested, be formed

around aircraft-carriers. But we have seen that a system of missile-ships linked to high-performance means of surveillance and search is also conceivable: this, like the aircraft-carrier group, would need surrounding protection. One can also envisage some forms of principal fighting force still further removed from the old battle fleets. SSNs could offer possibilities here, providing they had effective tactical communication links and weapons whose range was on a wide enough scale for them to reach the enemy effectively. Once such a fighting force has been assembled, decisions must be taken about where and when to deploy it, and this question will be examined later on with regard to combat between forces.

In sum, the problem of deployment appears, then, to involve some almost routine considerations and, in other respects, a crucial choice of options — which we are very conscious of having only touched upon — regarding the principal fighting force whose very existence, composition and purpose constitute the heart of the problem. It is, moreover, a problem of such magnitude that probably only the great navies have at their disposal sufficient means for them to have any choice in the matter.

Another unavoidable problem which will certainly always preoccupy a naval command at the start of hostilities is that of protecting assets at sea. European navies are still haunted by the importance that was attached to this during the last two world wars, when they were faced with a new weapon — the submarine. Today, since the vulnerability of industrial countries in relation to maritime transport has increased and submarines' potential has been magnified, this still appears to be one of the most important problems facing a naval command which is concerned with either defending or attacking commercial shipping.

We have seen, however, that the nuclear factor has changed matters in so far as an immediately convulsive total war would probably not allow time for a war on commerce to develop. But our research into the possibilities of naval warfare has equally made it evident, to our way of thinking, that a war on commerce could quite possibly take place as a preliminary to total war or as a prolongation of a total war that had been halted, or it could be waged during practically any kind of limited war, particularly if, by reason of the vulnerability of the countries concerned, there is an imbalance causing deterrence to be bypassed. Different kinds of scenario will, however, lead to very different kinds of war on commerce. During a prolongation of total war, the main concern would be survival, and shipping would be limited to the bare essentials (although it would be vital in a real sense); while in a limited war resulting from the bypassing of deterrence a nation with vulnerable seaborne trade would fight first of all to maintain economic prosperity and social calm and would thus keep its trade requirements at a high level.

All these considerations lead to one of the great difficulties of a war on commerce: nobody knows the facts in advance. We shall, however, attempt to open up some avenues for discussion. Let us put ourselves in the position of a power which takes the initiative in a war on commerce, that is to say which has decided on an offensive against enemy trade as a preliminary choice. The main problem is how to strike quickly and forcibly enough. Indeed, the result sought — the breaking down of the enemy by severing his supplies of all products — will be achieved only if the break is so savage and so rapid that the enemy has time neither to adapt himself to shortages nor to mount adequate defences. It is because these conditions were not met that so many wars on commerce failed in the past.

But to put all this into effect is not easy. In fact, the most favourable time for success would be in peace — gambling on surprise when merchant vessels are easy to find and defenceless along the shipping routes where they concentrate. But to achieve their destruction vast resources would need to be deployed; and there are many more merchant vessels in the world than ocean-going warships, particularly submarines. On the other hand, it is even more difficult today than before to keep a large deployment secret, even when only submarines are concerned, because absence from a port may less and less escape detection, just as a count of submarines in transit is one of the best possibilities for ground acoustic arrays. Nevertheless, the concentrated targets constituted by super-tankers today offer opportunities that are, to say the least, interesting, despite all the difficulties, which can be offset by exploiting the endurance of modern submarines in order to spread their deployment over a long period.

We must now put ourselves in the position of the nation under attack or, rather, to start a little further back in the process, the vulnerable nation that is fearful for its commercial supply lines. The first question to be answered is 'what must be defended?' This is a complex business: it is by no means as simple and clear-cut as on land. Is it sufficient to provide for just the needs of the fighting forces and the bare survival of the population, or for an economy in a state of growth and eager for raw materials? Should rationing be introduced by legislative measures? What stocks have been piled up? Where are the sources of supply, and can they be changed to make their defence easier? All these questions are at governmental and political level, and the military command has no control over them. For all that, they are no less crucial, and, in the situation we envisage, the naval command must certainly consider whether it should insist upon merchant traffic being reduced.

Supposing that merchant shipping is in fact reduced to a minimum, while requiring protection by whatever means and from whatever enemy, what is to be done? One of the options is retaliation. The idea here is that, faced with merchant vessels coming under attack, one retaliates by inflicting on the enemy a kind of eye-for-an-eye, tooth-for-a-tooth revenge. This solution could be attractive if several conditions were met. The first is that one is less vulnerable than the enemy; indeed, if one is more vulnerable and this exchange of pawns is prolonged, one will be the loser in the end. Secondly, of course, there must be suitable enemy targets to make revenge meaningful. In order for a strategy of retaliation to be effective, it must be clearly perceived and understood — which would imply proximity in time and space between the misdeed and the punishment such that there is a clear and unmistakable link between the victim of one and the victim of the other. However, the situations where all these conditions could be met would probably be special and rather limited. Retaliation may therefore be effective in a particular situation, but it does not seem to be the answer as a general rule.

In order to examine the more general situations, we need to go into more detail. First of all, what is the threat? The submarine threat immediately springs to mind. Against submarines, the first thing to do is to evaluate the extent of the threat in the usual way so as to gauge the exact measure of the problem. In fact, even with a large, modern fleet of submarines, no nation can achieve a threat of equal intensity over all the oceans. A study of transit times and a well-informed guess about submarine endurance will give a rough idea of the number of boats likely to be on patrol. In the same way, a study of the number of potential merchant-ship targets, the number of submarines liable to attack them, the number of weapons each submarine carries and the hit probabilities of these weapons will lead to an evaluation of the rate of attrition to be expected and will give some idea of the time available before the traffic stream is strangled. While on this subject, it is worth recalling what we said earlier about resorting to the deterrent; we did not linger on the subject because it was apparent anyway that it would only be the ultimate resort after all other methods had failed and that it would not be a problem for the naval command. Our purpose here is to deal with direct defence by naval means.

One overriding consideration, in our view, is that if the enemy starts a war on commerce he must be expecting a long war and it is therefore of the utmost importance to destroy his submarines in order to exhaust his potential for attack. One cannot rely on trying to escape them, as might be possible in a short war. It is necessary, therefore, to embark on an intensive ASW battle. Taking account of the difficulty of detecting submarines, one must, *a priori*, mount the battle at the three most favourable points — when the submarines are in their bases or are sailing from them, when they are passing through obligatory transit points (if these exist), and when they are closing on their targets which could, in this connection, be considered as a bait.

Attacking a base raises problems of principle, which we have already noted with regard to the option of attacking enemy territory. We shall come back to this in connection with mine warfare, which perhaps offers a way out of the dilemma. Attacking at obligatory points of passage is a classical choice, and modern techniques improve the chances of success. Attacking submarines in the vicinity of their targets implies, of course, that the latter must be well defended. This brings up the old question of convoys. Convoying would still seem to be a valid method of protection because the largest number of ships are protected by the least number of escorts and the latter are interposed between the assailant and his targets. Furthermore, the space available for protected ships inside a circle of protection increases in proportion to the *square* of the radius, whereas the circumference, where the escorts are positioned, increases only in proportion to the radius. But if the escort is to carry out its duties it must always remain with the convoy, even if its counter-attacks have not destroyed an attacking submarine. In order to destroy the submarine, after it has revealed its presence by an attack, it is just as necessary as in the past to have supplementary means of counter-attack. In view of the increased capabilities of submarines, however, the setting up of escorting forces and hunter-killer groups, together with the requirements for attacking bases and points of passage, will demand vastly greater resources than in the past.

One could say that the measures taken to reduce the amount of merchant transport required would lead to more effective protection of the shipping that maintains the flow — at least in the more hostile areas. But in fact this is unlikely to be the case, since there will always be a proportion of merchant ships that cannot be escorted. These will have to manoeuvre as necessary to evade submarines or at any rate to minimize losses. Evasion can no longer, however, be effected by simple course and speed changes such as zigzags and weaves, imposed on major routing and timing changes, which were the methods employed with regard to known or suspected submarine positions, to confuse submarines when submerged submarines were slower than merchantmen. With the appearance of SSNs there are no longer any 'limiting lines of approach' (the lines beyond which a submarine at a given speed cannot attain a firing position); an SSN can make its approach from any point on the horizon. Nevertheless, a submarine will have only a slight speed advantage over a good many modern merchant vessels. Thus, although it is impossible to prevent a submarine from attaining an attacking position, it may be possible to prevent it from torpedoing several ships during one attack, provided that its weapon range is not too great, by giving each ship sufficient sea-room in which to manoeuvre. This means that the faster vessels would be given carefully calculated courses and speeds that would keep them well apart so that one submarine hunting one particular unit might lose the rest of the group. Once merchantmen have approached their port of destination, however, they would have to close ranks and would then require even greater protection. It may be possible in the future to establish sanctuaries for arriving merchant ships by installing mobile and static acoustic arrays together with the appropriate ASW weapons. However, this in itself opens up another problem area: if the plan has not been fully carried out — if, in other words, the chances of successfully finding and attacking a submarine are not very high — a sanctuary becomes dangerous rather than useful because of the high concentration of potential targets in one area.

We now turn to examine the surface threat, which has a considerable potential for destruction because in general the weapons carried by each ocean-going surface unit enable it to tackle a wide variety of targets. Surface attacks are more limited than attacks by SSNs because surface ships are not faster and without nuclear propulsion they are less self-sufficient. On the other hand, the range of their weapons and their ability to detect and classify merchantmen are far superior. If it seems that the enemy has decided to use his surface forces against merchantmen, the same principle as applied to submarines will apply: enemy warships must be attacked and sunk. It is easier to attack surface ships than submarines because they are easier to find, and an escort is efficient here. Dispersion of shipping is less effective as a defence against surface ships because the latter's weapons have a larger radius of action than those of submarines. This suggests, even more strongly, that submarines must keep on the offensive if they are to have value for defence against the surface threat.

The air threat calls for very careful consideration. In basic terms, there are today, unlike in the past, plenty of aircraft with a radius of action that enables them to launch attacks from very long range. For example, there are bases within the USSR and the eastern European bloc from which aircraft could mount attacks against the western approaches to Europe and elsewhere. The size of the threat is considerable, as is the destructive potential, by virtue of the number of weapons a modern aircraft can carry which enable it, with its high speed, to attack several targets during one mission even if they are widely dispersed. Zigzags and weaves, from a merchantman's point of view, are useless for evading air attack. In real terms, armed resistance is the only possible solution; and the defence of a merchant ship requires a different approach from that of a warship which, because it is intended for fighting, merits the most effective method of self-defence which a modern guided-missile system can afford. But it can hardly be thought that this would be economically viable for merchant ships, bearing in mind that their normal activities by no means constantly expose them to an air threat. The only practicable solution is to provide naval units as anti-aircraft escorts. These could either be missile-armed ships or, even better, fighter aircraft capable of long-range interception. If a convoy is out of range of land-based aircraft, ship-borne aircraft would have to be used. The latter have, incidentally, greater flexibility and are more suitable for the task.

On the face of it, the problem of attacking or defending commercial assets at sea is highly complex and is attended by many unknowns. It must be emphasized, however, that it is only partly a military problem. It should therefore be studied by politicians and economists, if a clear picture of what should be defended is to be obtained. From the military point of view, the situation is very complicated because defences have to be prepared against any type of threat at sea. That merchantmen are extremely vulnerable to attack is unquestioned; yet it has always been the case that an effective war on commerce requires enormous and widely varied means of attack. But, if this is true, even greater means are required for defence. Attack is still the best means of defence and it would seem best for the defenders to adopt an extremely offensive attitude when seeking to destroy the aggressors, but they should also try to confuse attacks against them by judicious use of unpredictable course and speed changes.

The fifth operational problem is battle between naval forces. Battles may result from various different situations such as we have already discussed under one heading or another elsewhere in this study. Combat action could arise, for example, from an initial decision to take the offensive against an enemy force, to prepare a defence against such an offensive if one is in the opposite position, or to oppose an attack on territory or commercial assets; and combat would involve ships, aircraft, submarines or land-based weapons. Fighting could thus assume a multitude of forms and, above all, it could be nuclear. On the other hand, the conduct of operations depends on tactical considerations which are beyond the confines of our debate. In view of these factors, what conclusions can be drawn?

It would seem that the area where investigation would be most profitable, since it is the most recent and exhaustive, is that of a large-scale offensive between adversaries who have all the resources at their disposal, and with the possibility of nuclear warfare which could be initiated by either side. On the basis of what has already been discussed, one can imagine some of the features that would characterize a battle between naval forces, and it should be possible to suggest how the battle may be fought. The features that deserve particular attention are:

1 The battle will take place against a background of strategic deterrence.
2 Since effective means of early warning and reconnaissance will probably be available, each side will be well informed about the dispositions and movements of each other's surface units.
3 Knowledge and current intelligence about the capabilities and characteristics of the enemy's equipment and resources will not be as precise as in the past.
4 The battle will have a very technical character. Indeed, with self-guided missiles, the part played by the expertise of those who are fighting, in relation to that of the technicians who designed and produced the missiles, is decreasing. In addition, computerized information about the enemy would be of crucial importance.
5 Since the hit probability for a missile is far greater than with conventional gunnery systems, the advantage will undoubtedly lie with he who fires first.
6 Structural design and damage control will be of the utmost importance in the future, in order to ensure that a ship does not sink as the result of one missile hit.
7 It is important to try to choose a battlefield where land-based

aircraft and fixed acoustic arrays can, if possible, be used in support.

8 Certain submarines will be directly involved in action with surface and air units.

9 The speed of weapon carriers and weapon ranges will be just as important as they always have been; the ideal situation, of course, is to have the enemy within one's own reach while remaining outside his weapon range.

10 Battles will be fought in an electronic environment and this will be particularly true of weapons systems.

11 Morale and determination will be of even greater importance than in the past because, quite apart from their effect on battles themselves, they will play a direct role in deterrent manoeuvres.

The above considerations are very general but the following brief conclusions can be derived from them as to the way in which combat between naval forces will be conducted:

1 Ship formations will be designed with an eye to deception, while being suited to defence against nuclear attack.

2 The movements and 'overhead' periods of observation satellites must be taken into account in order to establish the times of possible exposure. If possible, ships should shift position at high speed immediately after the passage of a satellite to maintain uncertainty and continue to achieve surprise.

3 So far as possible, one must seek to remain outside the enemy's range, bearing in mind that permission to open fire may not immediately be given by the politicians.

4 Given range advantage, one must remain outside the enemy's range, closing only if one has inferior weapon range.

5 Choosing the battlefield may prove difficult because one will have to weigh the advantages of relatively well-protected inshore areas, where land-based aircraft and fixed acoustic arrays can give support, against a more forward position which is more likely to afford ascendancy over the enemy.

6 Since SSNs will be the only units capable of maintaining an element of surprise, it may well be that they will be able to play an advantageous role in co-ordination with other units.

7 It will be more important to sink ships than simply to disable them.
8 Since it is likely that true enemy capabilities will be learned only during an actual engagement, it will be very important to observe these precisely, with a view to possible future battles.

It will be useful to record the number of missiles fired by the enemy, because, if the rate of launching during any one engagement does not increase and the total number is not very great, it will be reasonable to assume that he is growing short of weapons and it may be possible to make an informed guess about the number of missiles he has left.

The whole subject of direct conflict between forces is by no means clear or predictable. It requires considerably more thought and research than it has so far been accorded.

The final area of operations to be examined is that of mine warfare. Its role in defence is of manifest importance; and the maintenance of free access to ports and anchorages is an obvious necessity. Technology in this field has advanced considerably and various new possibilities in the use of mines are now apparent, although the basic principles differ little from those of the past.

The most interesting aspect of mine warfare, and one that deserves some further brief discussion, is the use of mines in their offensive role. Aircraft with an increased radius of action and mines with an increased depth capability have added a new dimension to mine warfare. For the larger countries it has now become a practical possibility to lay mines in an enemy's ports and approaches as well as in navigationally restricted waters. It is also possible quickly to replace whatever mines the enemy has succeeded in sweeping. This therefore offers the means to exploit geographical irregularities to make the best use of the mine's potential. Although mine warfare is not entirely effective yet in deep water, it could be very profitable for closing off areas in confined waters and for restricting the enemy's freedom of movement. There is also an indirect benefit here in the delays that minefields impose on enemy movements.

Mine warfare might offer the naval command certain resources for overcoming the problem of attacking bases belonging to a nuclear-armed force when deterrence is still in play – especially during a crisis or at the outbreak of hostilities when the belligerents are already actively engaged in operations but have not yet resorted to strategic weapons. Mines laid in harbour approaches establish, in effect, a potential threat to the users of the harbour without actually amounting to an outright territorial assault. It is conceivable that, in the very special situations brought about by the concept of deterrence, one could use the threat of laying mines to force the enemy to make concessions, and so on. This kind of deferred offensive action, made possible by modern mine warfare, would thus seem to offer considerable strategic resources, especially against countries with little access to the open sea.

Having reached the end of this brief inquiry into the problems of operational planning and tactics in naval warfare, we are all too aware of having offered more questions than answers. Excluding those areas where we simply do not have enough knowledge, the explanation would seem to lie in the fact that not only is there an almost infinite number of conceivable situations and types of naval warfare, but there is also a multiplicity of technical changes and developments which have so far not been properly tested, in all their combinations, in an extensive war. The limited conclusions of this inquiry can be summarized as follows: The imminent revolution in search and reconnaissance will result in all sides becoming obsessed with the implications and requirements of early warning. SSBN operations, which are today essentially a matter of planning and careful technical preparation, will continue as such for a long time yet, if effective measures are taken to keep submarines up to date; but battles may eventually have to be fought in support of these operations.

The deployment of naval forces, which has always been a major problem for operational planners, includes aspects that are more or less routine, despite their importance, because they correspond to specific tasks. However, there is the problem of the composition of the principal fighting force to be considered: few navies can approach the question realistically but the ideal would seem to be an extension of the 'elementary naval unit' which must be capable of defending itself against any threat while retaining its offensive potential. It could consist of a powerful and flexible naval air group; or it could be based upon intelligent missiles (as far as we know such missiles do not yet exist) with adequate means of search and early warning; or it could even comprise a force of SSNs. There are many possibilities to be explored.

Protection of trade at sea is a problem that is all the more formidable because not all the facts are available: a valid solution for any one power requires all the surrounding political and economic factors to be considered in addition to the purely military aspects. So far as military considerations are concerned, a major conflict would tend to be widespread and lengthy, but it is unlikely that an enemy would be wholly successful in fighting a trade war because his forces, as well as the vulnerable commercial assets at sea, will be too widely dispersed. A power whose merchant shipping is highly vulnerable would probably not have the means to fight such a war. In defence, it will be a matter of finding ways of limiting the losses.

Battles between forces could occur in any number of ways: support for SSBN operations and the protection of trade are two examples. When warfare assumes its most complex form, with nuclear weapons being employed by both sides at sea, problems of deployment are increased by the unknowns involved. Some of the characteristics of nuclear engagements can be imagined, and some ideas can be formulated about their conduct, but they remain open to a great deal more study. All the same, it is clear that they will be dependent on overall governmental nuclear strategies. Like future plans for SSBN operations and protection for unescorted merchant shipping, battles between forces raise the question of favourable combat zones, where there would be semi-mobiles, facilities for locating the enemy and support from shore-based forces.

Mine warfare is now an important factor in operational planning because the possibilities for offensive mining have opened up a new dimension. In particular, mines could well provide the means to attack the naval bases of a nuclear-armed opponent without actually resorting to territorial assault.

These thoughts on the conduct of naval operations place in perspective the interdependence between the decisions that have to be made in advance, the decisions to be made at the start of operations and the effective conduct of those operations.

The importance of making the right decisions at the start is clear; and this means correctly choosing the type of confrontation that one wants to be capable of undertaking, which dictates the naval tools that will be required. Similarly, what we have called the fundamental choices to be considered at the start of operations cover a wide field for well-equipped navies. The most important decisions are whether to attack or defend, and which targets should be given priority. The ultimate criteria in decision making must take into account the influence of initial decisions on the final outcome of the confrontation. It must also be stressed that, at sea, however much preparation and planning has been done beforehand, the unexpected will often occur and many of the decisions will have to be made at the last minute. Furthermore, one must always be prepared for a lengthy operation, whether in a time of tension or in war, but remain at the ready to tackle each turn of events.

CONCLUSION

What impressions can be gained from the multitude of new developments that we have attempted to outline? First of all, it is clear that the range of political purposes that naval operations can serve has widened. In addition to participating in traditional military actions at various levels, navies now play a major part in the world-wide strategic nuclear balance of power, which involves not only the nuclear-armed states but all nations, in various degrees. Navies are also participating more and more in the measures that states are increasingly taking to protect their assets at sea, as the oceans' economic resources become more accessible.

Secondly, the range of confrontations that naval support of political objectives can bring about has widened at both ends of the ladder of violence. On the bottom rung, the mere presence and behaviour of forces at sea, in the almost permanent state of tension in the world today, play a role which new national sensibilities and present-day possibilities for the dissemination of information make more and more important and demanding. At the other extreme, on the top rung of the ladder, the naval component of a possible total war — the declaration of which would mean that deterrence had failed — would certainly be equipped for nuclear combat.

Our third impression arises from the study of the technical developments of the participants in naval warfare, which have also widened and diversified in range. Although no one can have everything, everyone can find the resources that are needed to support their political objectives, provided these are within the means of the country concerned. This does not necessarily imply that everybody will know exactly what is required. A major problem is that the complexity of certain 'key resources' in naval warfare has made it impossible for small, or even medium-sized, countries to have a little of everything: they must forego certain types of resources. Another difficulty is the uncertainty about what equipment may be developed in the future. For instance, can one be sure of what will happen in the fields of satellite and sonar surveillance?

Ultimately, then, the naval game remains interrelated with the technological explosions and the political changes that shake our world. It is very complex, highly technical, continually changing and very difficult, but it is also very important. Every state, therefore, must make clear decisions. The first choice is prior to the naval problem and concerns political objectives; this is obviously outside our field of study, but its significance must be underlined. It is this choice in particular which indicates both a country's ambitions and the margin for manoeuvre it has allowed itself. The second choice brings us into the field of naval action. It concerns the type and size of confrontation in which a naval force may be capable of involving itself in order to support political objectives; and the importance of making the right choice has already been emphasized several times. However, it should be noted that a great national ambition does not necessarily imply an ability to sustain the most intense confrontations. The choice must also take into account how the government envisages using its margin for manoeuvre. The third choice with a naval application concerns the scale of naval operations that one wants to be able to sustain, and how this compares with the capabilities of other countries (although much depends upon the general political and geostrategic scenario): where, for how long, with whom and against whom does one want to work?

More directly a naval concern is the vital point about what a navy should consist of, in relation to what it wants to do and what it is really capable of doing. We have tried to put forward some factors that might help to illuminate this decision, and we have shown the need for constantly testing and developing intelligence about the technical data that can be used to advantage. It should also be borne in mind that many problems are world-wide, that the breadth of certain weapons systems is also global, and that certain operations, like those concerned with the nuclear strategic balance, have a world-wide significance, even though only a few countries are pursuing them. Thus any given state is highly influenced by others' choices when making its own decisions: for example, if one state were to provide itself with a complete satellite reconnaissance system, whatever decisions another state made in this matter the movements of its large ships would thereafter be observed. What is required, therefore, is to look not only at one's own problems and decisions but also at those of other countries.

Finally, there are decisions to be made in purely operational matters, and these decisions assume increasing importance the higher one climbs up the intensity ladder. They have to be carefully considered in advance because, often enough, they must be taken into account well before the start of operations, from the moment when the naval arm is being defined. It is only possible, in practice, to lay down general guidelines and then tailor them to whatever situation evolves.

Thus decisions concerning a country's naval policy result from all kinds of factors affecting the national situation, as well as from an evaluation of purely naval factors at a particular point in time. In short, naval policy must be integral with the overall current military and political policies. Today, then, out of the dense and mysterious mists that conceal the sea from human view, a more and more distinct image of the future is emerging — one which is in some ways promising but also fraught with urgent demands and dangers. At every level in a competitive world the geostrategic importance of the sea keeps growing; and all the means are available to make use of it.

POSTSCRIPT: THE FALKLANDS WAR

This postscript was written, for this English edition, in the summer of 1982, because for the first time since the Second World War, we have seen an air and naval confrontation of considerable importance — the Anglo—Argentine conflict over the Falkland Islands. Unfortunately, there is not yet much professional information about the more technical aspects of this conflict, in which for the first time modern weapons have been used to a significant degree. In order to evaluate realistically the various aspects of these weapons, it would be necessary to have full data on the parameters of their systems, as well as their performance. Since these details will be fully available only in the long term, one must use caution and speak only in the broadest terms. And, of course, our concern here is only with the naval aspects.

To define this naval conflict in the terms used in this book, we can say that it involved *limited* naval warfare between a non-nuclear-armed force and a nuclear-armed force giving battle as a conventionally armed force. The stakes were territorial rights. The dispute occurred a considerable distance from the homeland of the victor; and the conflict was not very long. Although it concluded in a land battle, the conflict included a complete range of combined operations, among them being the transport of troops; the disembarkation of a landing force; naval fire support; logistic support; and action against naval and air forces, necessary to safeguard the unrestricted movement of equipment and materials as well as to deprive the enemy of his own freedom of action.

The Falklands war has demonstrated that naval warfare remains a viable possibility; but it is clear that this conflict was only one of several conceivable kinds of war and that sweeping conclusions should not be drawn from it. Another simple fact must be emphasized: despite the effect of losses on British morale and in spite of the courage of Argentine pilots, Britain still won the war.

Although Britain and Argentina have disputed territorial claims to the Falklands since the nineteenth century, it is rather curious that there was no period of mounting tension immediately before the conflict. Probably this was because the dispute had gone on for so long that the British government did not at first take this particular crisis too seriously. The operation was extended over a very large area, because the British units had to go from the Ascension Islands in order to reach the zone of conflict, a distance close to 4,000 nautical miles, with a long final approach during which there were many unknowns and a few brief encounters. Thus the majority of the more general 'classical' characteristics of a widespread maritime operation were seen in this confrontation.

The whole conflict has obviously raised some serious questions on the subject of early warning and search. It is a very sensitive area about which, unfortunately, we lack information. However, it is worth noting that, at a time of full hostilities, the British forces fitted out their huge Nimrod MPAs with in-flight refuelling, thus giving them the ability to operate as far as the Falklands; this was because of the urgent need for a means of search and hence early warning.

The length of time taken for the British task force to complete the final leg of its journey, and its standing-off period within the total-exclusion zone around the Falklands, demonstrated immediately the competence of underway logistic support in maintaining the self-sufficiency of a modern naval task force comprising some 40 naval units, as well as Great Britain's ability to provide the required supplies and stores on a continuing basis. Particular credit is due for the efficient way in which a commercial fleet was requisitioned and adapted for logistic roles.

Unfortunately, little is known about what we have called the final preparations before battle. Although we know a little more about the actions themselves, since some of the more basic details were immediately available as battles took place and casualties were incurred, none the less precise information is scant. Traditional weapons were certainly extensively used, as well as missiles and, most probably, electronic warfare. Missiles proved themselves to be effective. The importance of submarines was especially well illustrated although, employed so as not to be rendered detectable, they were not in the limelight. In fact, the deterrent effect of a single British SSN, leading to the sinking by torpedoes of the Argentine cruiser *General Belgrano*, was apparently sufficient to keep the Argentine surface fleet in its home waters for the duration of the conflict. It is also highly probable that the existence of the small Argentine submarine force caused the British admiral to take ASW precautions to such an extent that operations for repossession of the Falklands were considerably hampered and delayed.

The British aircraft-carriers played a most effective and spectacular role. From the Argentine point of view, the absence of their carrier *25th of May* from the battle area is notable. Without doubt this was wise, because the number of units that would have been required to provide an adequate protective screen were not available. From the British point of view, the carriers *Hermes* and *Invincible*, with their Sea Harrier aircraft and Sea King helicopters, undoubtedly formed the core of the task force, despite the fact that they were not catapult-fitted and had an incomplete complement of aircraft. It is remarkable, in view of the continual harassment from Argentine air attacks, that these aircraft-carriers were not immobilized. This demonstrated, again, that well-manoeuvred aircraft-carriers can escape attackers.

As to the value of the weapons package constituted by a light aircraft-carrier and its attendant aircraft, this will certainly be one of the more vigorous points of discussion for the future. Its opponents would have to prove that a large catapult-fitted aircraft-carrier, with a full-strength air complement and a more potent armoury, would have been capable of detecting and engaging the Argentine assailants at long range and minimizing British losses. Its supporters, however, would retort that the Sea Harriers gave a very flexible and creditable performance in support of the task force, in their roles both of ground attack and of aerial combat. This latter point was brought out by the British government in the European Parliament, where it was stated that the aircraft had been credited with 23 Skyhawk kills.

The surface warships were at the heart of the battle. They suffered some serious losses, but they brought down a large number of aircraft. The duel between aircraft and ships continues to be finely balanced, demanding very high standards of performance; and the defence of ships against aerial attack and damage control calls for more attention. Mine warfare does not seem to have played a major role in the Falklands. It would seem that the Argentinians lacked the ability to mine effectively all the Falklands waters, and thereby severely impede the British navy.

It is clear that fighter and bomber aircraft played a key role in initial British plans. Helicopters too were omnipresent, and, as already mentioned, the conversion of the Nimrods amply demonstrated the necessity of early warning and search, although the amount of information obtained was rarely sufficient. For instance, in the case of the *Sheffield*, which was successfully engaged by a Super Étendard aircraft, it is unlikely that she had sufficient warning of attack.

It may be said that the participants in this violent conflict surprised nobody; but the campaign gives rise to a long list of questions which are bound, at least, to stimulate curiosity, and the conduct of operations in the Falklands war will certainly provide a wide variety of subjects for future debate within military colleges.

We shall not attempt to discuss the decisions taken after deployment of the British task force, but it is worth briefly considering the choices that were available in advance, and, above all, the fundamental question that arises: were the naval tools of the belligerents adequate to support the political aims of their governments? So far as Argentina is concerned, the answer is no. The Argentine navy is close-knit and fairly powerful, as was the air force, although this is now much weakened by losses. Did senior Argentine leaders believe, perhaps, that Britain would not physically oppose an invasion of the Falklands? If so, the error was political. In every way Argentina involved itself in an operation for which it did not have adequate military means.

Britain's position is more complicated. The United Kingdom still has one of the most powerful military forces in the world; but, although Britain won this war, the losses incurred and the measures taken imply that British forces encountered difficulties that were more serious than originally thought. The roles that successive governments had assigned to the British navy over the past few years had all resulted in a significant cutback in equipment and resources, including cuts in ship-borne aircraft. The Falklands operation was an ambitious, long-distance project; and the reductions in ship-borne aircraft cost dearly. Doubtless there were political reasons for the shortage of naval equipment, but the global strength of the standing British forces and the vigour and speed with which they called up their extra resources compensated for this. It is probable, too, that the threat was underestimated in some quarters, with the result that military force was used only after the Falklands had been invaded by Argentina. It is very possible that a few well and timely deployed warships would have been sufficient to deter any likely invader.

These few general thoughts on some of the aspects of modern naval warfare in the light of the Falklands conflict may be of interest in years to come. However, a further point must be made: the most important single factor is the dedication and sheer courage of the men who fight. Dedication, patriotism and pride played an important role in the Falklands war, with support for their governments being shown by the populations of both countries. It was a paradoxical case — two Western nations in arms against each other. The courage shown on both sides was unquestionable. In the harsh climatic conditions of the South Atlantic, the best equipment would have been useless if not served by alert, determined, patient and brave men. A spectator from afar can do no better than end by paying homage to the qualities displayed by the men involved on both sides of a bitter confrontation.

INDEX

Page numbers for main entries are in italic type; plate numbers are in bold type.

acoustic arrays 52—3, 120
  fixed ground 52—3, 63, 64, 68, 77, 97, 98, 111
  towed 63
  see also sonar
acoustic warfare 99
aircraft 16, *74*, 132, 133, 134
  ASW 63
  -carriers & carrier-borne aircraft 21, 55, *68—71*, 114, 126, 133—4, **1**, **2**, **4**, **7**, **14—15**, **29**, **33—4**, **36**, **52**; offensive capabilities 69; vulnerability 70—1
  maritime-patrol 51, 74, 98
  mine-laying 73
  see also helicopters
amphibious craft **18**, **23**
anti-submarine warfare *62—8*, 106—7, 118—20, 133, **14—15**, **39**, **50**, **61**
  detection 62—3, 65, 72
  see also submarines; undersea warfare
assault craft **18**, **20**, **23**
assets, maritime, *see* commercial assets at sea
ASW, *see* anti-submarine warfare

battles, *see* naval battles
bulk transporters 47

Captor 64
coastal defence 96—7
command 20, 41, **10**, **14—15**
commercial assets at sea 15—16, 21—2, 47—8, 77, *115—21*, 126, **39**
  offensive action against 108—9
  protection against submarines 66—7, 117—20
  protection by nuclear deterrence 38, 43—4
  see also merchant vessels
communications systems 19, 20, 59, **14—15**
computer systems **25**, **38**
concentration, capacity for 81
confrontations 9—11, 19, 34—5, 36—7, 82, 92—3; *see also* crises, continual; war
constraints 20, 35
containerization 47
control of the sea 14—15, 18
convoying 118—21, **21—2**, 56
  anti-aircraft escorts 121, **4**

crises, continual 17—18, 34—5, 78—83, 103—4, 135; *see also* nuclear crisis

data processing 59, **78**
deployment of forces 19—20, 113—15, 125—6
detection, *see* intelligence; passive listening; sensors; anti-submarine warfare; *and specific equipment, e.g.* acoustic arrays
deterrent naval elements 17—18, 135; *see also* nuclear deterrence
disembarkation of landing forces 13
distance, an operational characteristic 35, 93—4, **27**

economic interests, *see* commercial assets at sea
electronic warfare 58—9, 99, **3**, **33**
equipment, improvements in 37, 51—9
escort **4**, **7**, **19**, **56**
explosives, conventional 40

Falkland Islands conflict (1982) 10n, *131—5,* **1**, **11**, **23**, **27—9**, **31—2**, **34—6**, **51**, **65**, **72**
ferries, drive on/drive off 47
fire support from seaward 13—14
flexible response 11
force-de-frappe 11

gas propulsion **3**
geographical characteristics of the marine environment 31
geographical factors of naval warfare 106
  influence of technical developments on 76—7
guns 55—6, 58, **21—2**, **72**, **77**

harassment 17—18, 34—5, 78—83, 103—4, 135
helicopters 55, 73, *74—5*, 133, 134, **21—2**, **27**, **51—7**, **65—6**
  ASW 64, **10**, **13**, **53—4**, **57—8**, **61**, **81**
homing devices, and conventional explosive warheads 40, **32**

innovations 37, 51—9
intelligence
  an operational characteristic 35
  -gathering operations 18, 19, 34, 51—3, 111—12, 132, 134
  see also specific systems, e.g. maritime-patrol aircraft

jamming, anti-jamming **38**

landing craft **18**, **20**
legal aspects of the marine environment 31—2
legal position of naval officers 33
limited war, *see* war, limited
logistic support 14, 53, 69, **16**, **27**

magnetic anomaly detection equipment (MAD) 55, 63, 74, **57**
marine environmental elements 31—2, 39
  significance in a nuclear battle 41
merchant vessels 15—16, 21, 47, 115—21, 126, **28**, **77**
  air threat to 120—1

convoying 118—20
offensive action against 108—9, 116
protection against submarines 66—7, 117—20
protection by nuclear deterrence 38, 43—4
size & speed increases 47
surface threat 120
vulnerability 47
minehunters *73—4*, **9**
mines 73, 97, 124—5, 126
minesweepers 73
missile-attack craft 96—7, 115, **73**
missiles *56—8*, 133, 134, **3**, **21**, **49**
and new operational possibilities 96—7
air-to-air **32**
air-to-surface 58, **30—1**, **51**, **74**
anti-missile defence 58, 65, 100—1, 7, **10**, **13**, **62**, **64**, **74**, **77—9**
anti-ship missiles 101, **56**, **64**, **65—6**, **69—71**, **76**, **78**, **80**
as warship firepower 72—3, **63—4**
ASW 64, **46**
cruise 39, 57, 72, **46**, **48**, **69**, **75**
in future 82
SSBN 21, 24, 65—6, 112, **44**, **67**
surface-to-air 72, **13—15**, **18**, **62**, **75**, **79**
surface-to-surface 56—7, 76, 77, **13—15**, **48**, **58—60**, **74**, **76**
mobility 51—3, 76

naval arm, role of *13—16*
naval bases overseas 47, 94
naval battles
in future 59, 121—4, 126
and weapons systems 55—9
naval command, constraints on 20
and use of nuclear weapons 41
naval confrontations, *see* confrontations
naval forces
composition of principal force 114—15, 125, 129—30
deployment of 19—20, 113—15, 125—6
minimum size 77—8, 95, 125—6
a stake for naval action 16, 22
naval operations *89—127*
and nuclear defence 40—1
choices to be made in advance *91—102*
context of *37—48*
diversity of 15
general characteristics *31—6*, 78
key resources 77, 86—7, **5**, **20**, **37**, **76**
options at the start *103—9*
place of naval operations today *17—27*
problems *110—27*
see also nuclear weapons
naval policy, conclusions *128—30*
naval strategy 38—9, 48, 51—3, 61, 65—8, *76—85*, 95—8; *see also* mobility, nuclear weapons
naval units
elementary naval unit 78, 95, 125—6
list of key requirements 87
see also specific units, e.g. minehunters
nuclear crisis 19—20, 78—9, 83
nuclear deterrence 37—9, 79
and naval strategy 38—9, 48

and protection of commercial maritime interests 38, 43—4
and tactical nuclear weapons 41—2, **49**
see also SSBNs
nuclear propulsion 53, 60, **7**, **14—15**
nuclear virginity 41, 42, 108, **30**
nuclear war 10, 11, 21—3, 83—4
nuclear weapons *37—45,* 107—8, 109, 112, **30**, **67**
use of, at sea 39—43, 100, **44**
ASW 64
political constraints, 41, 42
see also missiles

offensive action 105—9, 116
oil rigs 48, **39**
oil tankers 47, 116

passive listening 54—5, 62—3
peacetime show of force, 17—18, 34—5, 78—83, 103—4, 135, **17**
political objectives 128—30, **17**; *see also* peacetime show of force
political pressure 18
principal naval force, composition of 114—15, 125, 129—30
principles of war 104—5
effect of technical developments on 78—82

radar 51, 57—8, 74, **38**, **52**, **59**, **70**, **72**, **75**, **78**
resources
needed in naval operations 77—8, *86—7*
effects on principles of action 81—2
use of 19—20, 113—15, 125—6

satellites
communications 59
naval surveillance 52, 70, 98—9, 111, 112
sea-to-shore action **5**, **29**, **72**
search and reconnaissance 51—3, 98—9, 111—12, 125
list of key requirements 86
see also specific systems, e.g. satellites; acoustic arrays
sensors 19, 54—5, 60—1, 62—3, 86; *see also specific equipment, e.g.* radar
ships, *see* aircraft-carriers; anti-aircraft convoy escorts; merchant vessels; mine-hunters; minesweepers; warships
shore-to-sea action 76—7
sonar 55, 61, 62, **26**, **54**, **57**; *see also* acoustic arrays
sonic detection, low frequency 63
sonobuoys 63, 74, **57**
Soviet navy 73, **10**, **14—19**, **41**, **49—50**
SSBNs 21, 24, 39, 60, 61, 65—8, 84, **44—5**, **47**, **67**
and second strikes 38—9
operational principles 112—13, 125, 126
see also missiles, SSNs
SSNs 60, 61, 81, 83, 115, 119, 126, 133, **11**, **14—15**, **46**, **50**
stakes for naval action 15—16, 21, *46—8*
strategy, *see* naval strategy
submarines *60—8,* **40—50**, **68**, **70**, **80**
ballistic missile, nuclear, *see* SSBNs
diesel electric 62, **40—2**, **48**
nuclear-propelled attack-class, *see* SSNs
threat to aircraft carriers 71

threat to commercial interests at sea 66—7, 117—20
threat to naval forces 67—8, 72
threat to territory 65—6
see also anti-submarine warfare; undersea warfare
super-tankers 116
surveillance 18, 19, 34, 51—3, 111—12, 132, 134, **37—8**, **52**, **56**, **75**; *see also* satellites

targets, choice of priorities 106—9
technical developments affecting naval warfare 37, 51—9, 76—8; *see also specific naval units, e.g.* warships
telecommunications, *see* satellites
telegraphy 59; *see also* communications systems
tension, low 17—18, 34—5, 78—83, 103—4, 135
territories
naval offensives against 107—8
vulnerability 46—7, to SSBN attack 65—6
time 35, 77, 94
torpedoes 56, **21—2**, **43**, **45**, **48**, **73**
ASW 56, 64, **13**, **46**, **53**, **57**, **61**, **80—1**
total war 10; *see also* nuclear war
transport of land forces 13, 21, **28**
troops 13, 14, 21, **18**, **20**

U-boats 60, **43**; *see also* submarines
undersea warfare 65—8, 118—20; *see also* anti-submarine warfare; submarines
urbanization 46

violence levels 7, 9
vital interests 44

war
aims 8—9
and humanity *7—12*
criterion of effectiveness 9
definition 7
duration of 10—11
in space 82
intensity of 9—10
limited 10, 23—6, 83—4, 131—5, **1**, **5**
nuclear, *see* nuclear war
total, *see* nuclear war
see also confrontations
warheads, *see* explosives nuclear weapons; weapons systems
warning systems **10**, **33**
warships 32—3, 40—1, 53, 63—4, 67—8, 71—3, 134, **5**, **6**, **13**; *see also* weapons systems; *specific types, e.g.* minehunters
weapons systems *55—9*, 86, 98—102, **25**, **34**; *see also specific systems, e.g.* guns; missiles